BREAKTHROUGH
ON
THE COLOR FRONT

To Ray & Sheila Hiebert

with warm best wishes,

& memories....

[signature]
Washington, D.C.
November 18, 1993

BREAKTHROUGH ON THE COLOR FRONT

Augmented Edition

LEE NICHOLS

With Foreword by
Lt. General Benjamin O. Davis, Jr.,
and Author's Update on Current Status of
African Americans in the U.S. Military

Three Continents Press

Augmented Edition of 1993

Three Continents Press, Inc.
P.O. Box 38009
Colorado Springs, CO., 80937-8009

Library of Congress Cataloging-in-Publication Data
Nichols, Lee.
 Breakthrough on the color front / Lee Nichols with foreword by Lt. General Benjamin O. Davis, Jr. — Rev./Augm. ed.
  p. cm.
 Includes bibliographical references and index.
 ISBN 0-89410-771-2 : $24.00. ISBN 0-89410-772-0 : $15.00
 1. United States — Armed Forces — Afro-Americans. I. Title.
UP418.A47N43 1993
355'.0089'96073—dc20

93-24153
CIP

Dedication:

To all those who made possible what former President Harry S. Truman called "the greatest thing that ever happened to America" — the ending of segregation in the U.S. armed forces.

Lt. General Benjamin O. Davis, Jr.

21 May 1993

Mr. Lee Nichols
111 S. Adams Street
Rockville, MD 20850

Dear Mr. Nichols,

Thanks for writing about the republication of your book, Breakthrough on the Color Front. Congratulations on your latest project. I appreciate the kind words about my military career and your interest in my contributing to the new edition.

In response to your question about integration in the U.S. military, I believe my remarks to The National Association of Black Journalists in New York City on August 17, 1989, best delineate my thoughts on the subject. A copy of those remarks and several other speeches are enclosed. I hope you will find them and the copy of the Department of Defense publication, Black Americans in Defense of Our Nation, helpful for your research.

Best wishes for the book's success.

Sincerely,

COLIN L. POWELL
Chairman
of the
Joint Chiefs of Staff

In his remarks to the National Association of Black Journalists on July 11, 1991, General Powell said that:

"The armed forces of the United States affords the opportunity for advancement [for blacks and women] that, regrettably, is not in every part of our society . . . the kind of opportunity that the armed forces have led the way with and hopefully will eventually spread to all parts of our society so that only achievement and performance will be the basis for advancement . . . my generation in the military [is] a generation where almost all barriers have now dropped. . . ."

Acknowledgments

Any success that my original book, and this augmented edition, may have had or may enjoy, is due not only to my efforts but to a large number of persons and organizations who have inspired and helped me.

First of all I would like to pay tribute to the late James C. Evans, an African American and adviser on race relations in the Department of Defense in the 1950s, for tipping me off with a "wink and a nod" that something momentous was happening in the field of military racial change. While Evans was inhibited from giving me, as a United Press reporter, any direct information about the then-radical moves toward racial integration taking place in the military, his hints, and his assistance at every turn when I began cracking the military's silken curtain of secrecy on the subject, were incalculable in motivating and guiding me in my original efforts.

My thanks to the late President Truman, who told me personally of his motivation in moving toward integration of the armed forces and said he considered the achievement of that goal "the greatest thing that ever happened to America." I owe a debt of gratitude to the late General George C. Marshall, former Army Chief-of-Staff and later Secretary of State, and to a vast array of military officials, high and low, who gave me their personal views and helped me with my research once the Defense Department decided to open its doors and files to me. I recall particularly an Army public affairs officer, whose name I have long forgotten, who turned the key unlocking the Pentagon's door to its closely-held secret of ongoing integration, evidently convinced that the story had to be told and that I was a responsible journalist.

My heartfelt gratitude and long-overdue tribute to the late Neil MacNeil (Sr.), former assistant managing editor of *The New York Times*, who convinced me that I "owed it to America" to write my book, and who secured an agent who "sold" the book to Random House; and to MacNeil's son, Neil MacNeil, then a colleague at the UP (later UPI), who encouraged me and took me to meet his father at their home in Southampton, Long Island, where his father motivated me to write my first-ever book.

For this current "augmented" edition, I owe a debt of gratitude to military officials, including General Colin Powell, Chairman of the Joint Chiefs of Staff, and to a number of individuals and organizations outside the military who offered me their comments and criticisms on the current state of racial relations in the military.

I have an unforgettable debt to Lt. Gen. Benjamin O. Davis, Jr. (ret.), the first general officer in the U.S. Air Force, who played a significant part (not heretofore acknowledged in my book) in helping to integrate the Air Force, for his kind words about my book as reflected in his gracious Foreword to this edition.

I also thank my editors at Random House who gave me wise counsel and guidance, and almost last but not least, my wife Eleanor who typed my original manuscript and endured my acerb reaction to her criticisms of my writing — nearly all of which proved to be well-taken.

And I thank my friend and publisher of this edition, Donald E. Herdeck, for urging me to republish my book and helping me with encouragement and useful suggestions to get the job done.

Foreword

I reread Lee Nichols' *Breakthrough on the Color Front* recently and had the privilege of talking at some length to the author. The book is an even more valuable read today, in 1993, than it was almost forty years ago, when it was first published. Today, it is vitally important military history, not to be found anywhere else, to my knowledge, to the degree that it is consolidated and concentrated in the interesting and detailed presentations in this book.

The book starts in 1953 with exciting stories of combat with a number of life-and-death actions involving white and black military men, actions demonstrating mutual support and willing cooperation, despite the pattern of racial segregation that had dominated the U.S. military throughout its existence.

Nichols jumps very early on to a statement that the integration of the armed forces was spearheading an accelerated shift away from racial segregation throughout our nation. Most importantly, he points out the fact that in 1953, only five years after President Truman's Executive Order providing for "equality of treatment and opportunity" in the armed forces, blacks and whites were eating together, living in the same barracks, going to church and movies together, and living a common social relationship in base military clubs, swimming pools and other government facilities.

Nichols cites some of the main contributors to this revolutionary change — Presidents Roosevelt and Truman, Secretary of the Navy James V. Forrestal, and Secretary of the Air Force Stuart Symington. Lester Granger in the Navy and General Idwal Edwards in the Air Force are named as effective players, who took the critical timely actions that made things happen.

Also, in the Air Force, the stellar combat performance of the Tuskegee Airmen in World War II appealed strongly to many people who previously had doubted the ability of blacks to perform effectively in battle. Without any question, the rapidity and efficient movement of the Air Force toward integration in a very short period of months acted as a catalyst to move all of the armed forces much more rapidly toward the equal opportunity and treatment that President Truman's 1948 Executive Order had mandated for members of the armed forces. As early as 1950, the entire United States Air Force was living and convincing proof to the large numbers of earlier nonbelievers in the Army, the Navy, and the Marine Corps that integration might well be the best course to follow. Again, the role of the Tuskegee Airmen cannot be overemphasized as an important example of black military performance.

In addition, strong command leadership from the top down through all levels and parts of the military establishment was the other factor that made the program a success. Nichols properly compliments the Navy upon its progress toward integration. He recognizes the fact that the major integration problem, of course, rested with the Army, whose top leadership appeared resistant to compliance. Regardless of all attendant problems, however, Nichols' quote of President Truman's short, concise statement is the clincher that said it all: "It's the greatest thing that ever happened to America."

President Truman felt strongly that our nation was approaching a point where race superiority would no longer exist, where people would recognize that the human animal was the same, with the same feelings and emotions, no matter what the skin color. It is surely significant that only a few years after President Truman's order, Thurgood Marshall was successful in convincing a unanimous Supreme Court that our nation's public schools should be desegregated, because of the permanent psychological damage a segregated school system was inflicting upon the nation's black children.

Lee Nichols fills the remainder of his book with detailed, concrete examples of white-black on-base and off-base personal relationships throughout the United States, resulting directly from the integration of our armed forces. Though not stated directly and concisely, the inference is clear that an integrated military force is far more effective than any segregated force could possibly be. Proof of increased effectiveness was found both in the forces deployed to fight the Persian Gulf War, as well as in the military forces on bases in the United States.

Unfortunately, today, racism, segregation, hatred, separatism among groups of Americans, abound in our population. The military achieved its improved posture, as Nichols has demonstrated, through indoctrination training of its people in compliance with an executive order. No president can issue a similarly effective executive order to our civilian population. But voluntary training of pre-school children with parents and teachers in a structured national program, over a period of several decades, can, at the very least, start a move away from the hate and racism that make impossible the development of the happy, productive lives our citizens deserve. This type of attention to our shameful un-American national problem is warranted because of its demonstrated importance within our society. With all its faults, today, America is a far better nation than formerly. It's still, by far, the greatest nation in the world, and it's a nation that has room to develop better relationships among all of its people. Lee Nichols' book showed how it was done in the military; it would surely be good to see the same type of improvements throughout our society.

April 7, 1993

Lt. Gen. Benjamin O. Davis Jr. (retired). First black general in the U. S. Air Force. Leader of the Tuskegee Airmen, the first black fighter outfit that saw action in World War II; played important role in integrating the Air Force.

Author's Note for the New Edition of *Breakthrough on the Color Front*

Forty years have elapsed since I finished the last chapter and sent to the publisher my book on the integration of the U.S. armed forces, *Breakthrough on the Color Front.* I have been encouraged to republish the book for the following reasons:

The book, originally published in 1954, has long been out of print. The publisher, *Random House,* has no copies available for purchase. I have been unable to locate any copies among rare and old book search firms.

Breakthrough, as originally published, is valuable for a number of reasons. It records, authentically and for the first time, the integration of the U.S. armed forces — the ending of segregation of African American and white military personnel — which was nearly complete when the book was published. It is a historic

document. Equally important, it records the state of racial relations in the U.S. armed forces, both within the military establishment and in its relation to the civilian community, shortly before
the U.S. Supreme Court outlawed racial segregation in American
public schools.

It is for that reason that my present publisher, Three Continents Press, and I decided to republish the original text exactly as
it was first issued. We recognize that many elements of the
original book are outdated. For example, the wiping out of segregation had not been 100 percent completed at the time of publication. There were problems with off-duty mixing of Negro and
white servicemen on military posts, chiefly in the South, and
with nearby communities. (I am including an updated summary
of the present situation of blacks in the U.S. military as Appendix C.)

Nevertheless, the history of the utilization of Negro manpower in the U.S. military from the Revolutionary War down to
the Korean War, and the actual process of the integration of
black and white military personnel, are facts and, with a possible
few exceptions due to later research and information, part of the
record of the U.S. military establishment.

With current problems of race relations in the United States,
and the controversy over homosexuals in the military, the publisher and I feel that a revisitation of the military scene in the
early 1950s may offer significant insights.

There are sharply divergent points of view as to whether there
are parallels between the integration of African Americans and
the acceptance of homosexuals in the military. I will not attempt
to take sides in this argument except to note that my book
illustrates, with extensive factual reporting and reference to socio-
logical studies made in that period (1951-53), that (A) there was

widespread apprehension that mixing the races in training, duty, eating and sleeping arrangements and other aspects of military life would cause revulsion, even rioting and bloody revolution among white military personnel and the outside community; and (B) that almost universally *none of those fears was realized*: white soldiers, sailors, marines and airmen (and women) accepted mixing with black Americans for the most part calmly and, in many cases, gladly.

In my book I raised the question of whether the integration of the U.S. military would have any impact on American society as a whole. I concluded, based on instances cited in the book, comments by military officials and my own speculation, that it would inevitably affect the racial equation in American society. For one thing, I predicted that the desegregation of the U.S. military was a road from which there would be "no turning back." This has proved to be the case.

I cannot attempt here to reanalyze this question. I can state a few facts. Copies of most of the chapters of my book, still in manuscript form and as yet unpublished, were requested by two Supreme Court justices from the then-racial adviser to the Department of Defense, James C. Evans. This was at the time when the Court was weighing the school segregation case. Evans informed me of those requests and told me he had furnished the two justices with the manuscripts (which I had sent Evans for comment). He told me one of the justices was then-Chief Justice Fred Vinson, who died before the Court rendered its school desegregation verdict in May, 1954. Evans, now deceased, refused to tell me the name of the other justice who received the manuscript. These are facts. I have no knowledge of why the justices requested the manuscript or what, if any, influence it had on their deliberations in Brown vs. Board of Education.

I do know that the Department of Justice, in its *amicus curiae* brief to the Supreme Court urging the Court to implement its 1954 desegregation ruling, cited my book *by name* as containing evidence that desegregation could be accomplished without disruption of the U.S. social fabric.

The book was widely and prominently reviewed. It was known to many organizations seeking to promote racial equality in areas of civilian life. Whether the book and the military racial solution it depicted have had any impact on the civil rights struggle in the U.S. is for others to judge. As for me, a journalist, I simply reported what I discovered.

Following publication of my book, I played a part in the integration of public schools in Montgomery County, Maryland, my home; and was publicity director of Suburban Maryland Fair Housing, a volunteer organization seeking to end segregated housing in Washington's Maryland suburbs.

Lee Nichols was co-sponsor, with Drew Pearson and Marquis Childs, of the first African American admitted to membership in the National Press Club of Washington, D.C.

CONTENTS

APPENDICES

List of Illustrations and Documents

(Placed between pages 214 and 215 except for General Davis, Jr.)

more

Author's Note

A seemingly casual army press release and the guarded words of a Pentagon official started me on a trail that led, through offices of military and political leaders, through secret files and military bases, to what may turn out to be one of the biggest stories of the Twentieth Century.

It was so big, in fact, that it could never be told even in a series of news dispatches, although the United Press, for which I have been proud to work for a dozen years, has carried "bites" of it. To cover the whole play of events took a book; and I was literally forced to write it when I saw how important were the facts involved and their implications for my fellow Americans, perhaps for all mankind.

Working on the UP night desk in Washington, I have spent most of my days, week-ends and holidays for over a year interviewing hundreds of officials, from former President Truman, Generals Marshall and Bradley and Admiral Denfeld to lesser known but pivotal officials who played leading roles in the drive to end military racial segregation.

Fortunately I tackled the subject at just about the time the military, particularly the cautious Army, was ready to lift the curtain of secrecy and let the story be told. Assured that the subject would be handled objectively and fairly, officials of all services gave me access to a wealth of secret documents not hitherto made public. In addition, I have visited army, navy, marine and air force bases from Washington, D.C., to Biloxi, Mississippi, observing the non-segregation program and questioning commanders, post officials and servicemen—Negro and white.

It will take future historians, with access to still unavailable records, personal letters, etc., to evaluate precisely the many diverse factors that have made possible the successful military racial revolution of the past ten years.

I have talked to almost every key person available who was concerned with the racial integration program; have studied all accessible records; and have checked my findings by personal interview or correspondence with others in a position to evaluate the conclusions.

It is perhaps inevitable, in this type of work, that some who were involved will think too much emphasis was put on the "chiefs" in one case, or on the "Indians" in another; they may be right in part. The author was limited, partly by the death or wide scattering of military personnel, in reaching everyone deeply involved in the non-segregation program. Thus where "chiefs" were the main source of information they may have received greater emphasis, since they would naturally see things from their vantage point; but the "Indians," as men in less prominent but often crucial positions are wont to style themselves, likewise became leading actors where they were the prime informants.

In dramatizing such persons, or certain aspects of the program, I am not attempting to make value judgments as to who did what but only to tell the story, as accurately yet as colorfully as possible, according to the way I got it. Further facts may later lead to new light on some aspects of the broad development encompassed in this brief volume.

I have largely avoided the use of footnotes which tend to disturb the general reader, for whom this book is chiefly intended. Where possible I have included references in the body of the text. To the few absolutely essential notes I have added a bibliography at the end of the book which shows the source of factual material not otherwise accounted for, with one main exception: where official military documents are quoted, I have not always felt it necessary to name the source, since they *are* official records, and in many cases were given to me on a confidential basis. Thus, the social science research studies of the Army's integration program, referred to in Chapter XIII and elsewhere, are still in a "secret" category and were made available to me only on condition that I should not name the source.

Nearly all quoted remarks of living persons, where not otherwise indicated, were made in interviews with the author, who wishes to acknowledge gratefully the kindness of many busy men of high and low station who took time to help provide pieces for this monumental jigsaw puzzle.

In almost every case the material thus supplied has been checked against the sources, and their corrections and suggestions have been largely incorporated.

There were several minor problems in writing about military subjects for non-military readers. I have tried, wherever possible, to reduce military language to the generally familiar. One question was what to do about the rank of military men who later advanced to higher rating. To simplify matters, I have customarily used the rank held at the time of the incident described.

Finally, I must give grateful thanks to my wife, my colleagues and my friends, whose encouragement and active help in criticizing, reading manuscript and typing have made an impossible task possible; and above all, to the public information officers of all services, in the Pentagon and at bases, North and South, without whose magnificent cooperation in getting at officials and official material this book could not have been written.

LEE NICHOLS
(1953)

Breakthrough on the Color Front

ONE

The Unknown War

On the battlefields of Korea, on America's fighting ships and planes and at its bases at home and abroad, a victory has been forged in one of the most significant social wars in the nation's history.

It was fought with so little fanfare that few knew it was going on, and the magnitude of its success has only begun to become apparent — an achievement in human relations not anticipated for decades, perhaps a century or more.

It could be a sign that man's neglected art of learning to live in dignity and peace with his neighbor was at last beginning to catch up with his strides in the science of destruction.

Perhaps the best way to envisage the new pattern emerging within the military realm is to focus on specific episodes.

On December 5, 1950, a squadron of U.S. Navy planes from the aircraft carrier *U.S.S. Leyte,* off Korea, was bombing and strafing Chinese Communist troops in the battle of the Chosin Reservoir.

One of the navy planes was hit and went down. Crashlanding in a rough field five miles in front of the American lines, it burst into flames.

The pilot of a companion plane, spotting the burning craft, landed nearby and ran to the rescue. Unable to open the canopy to get the pilot out, he packed the fuselage with snow to keep the fire back. A marine helicopter landed with axes and rescue equipment, but was too late to save the flier, who died in the pyre of his plane.

The pilot who died was Ensign Jesse L. Brown, officially listed as the first Negro pilot in navy history. The man who risked death or capture to save him was Lieutenant (j.g.) Thomas J. Hudner, a white pilot, who was awarded the Medal of Honor for his heroism.

On June 2, 1951, a platoon officer of Company C, 24th Infantry Regiment, 24th U.S. Division, was wounded during an attack on a Communist-held hill near Chopo-ri, Korea. A twenty-one-year-old sergeant assumed command of the platoon, led a handful of men up a steep hill and personally wiped out two enemy positions with grenades and rifle fire, killing six enemy soldiers.

Devastating enemy fire was coming from heavily fortified automatic weapon emplacements. The sergeant regrouped his men and led them in a rush to the top of the hill. A rain of grenades staggered the charge. The sergeant was wounded. Refusing medical aid, he led his men in another charge. Again it met a shower of grenades.

A third time the sergeant rallied his men, rushing the hilltop to find that the main enemy gun position holding back the attack was on the reverse slope. Bleeding heavily from a jagged chest wound, he charged the position alone. Another grenade exploded at his feet, mortally wounding him. With his last bit of strength, he fired a burst from his weapon and silenced the enemy strong point.

For this, Sergeant Cornelius H. Charlton, a twenty-one-year-old Negro from the Bronx, was given the Medal of Honor after death. The officer whose place he took was a white man. The men of the platoon were Negroes and whites, mixed indiscriminately.

In the Army's Walter Reed Hospital in Washington, D.C., a young soldier waiting to be fitted with an artificial left foot described how he was wounded on Sniper Ridge in Korea in the late summer of 1952.

An enemy grenade exploded in his bunker just as he tried to kick it away. When no medical corpsmen answered his cries, he crawled to the bunker of his squad leader, a sergeant, who applied a tourniquet and watched over him in spare moments while directing the squad in repulsing a savage, two-hour attack.

The soldier, Private First Class Donald T. Young, a white man from Roanoke, Virginia, said his sergeant, a Negro, had written to find out how he was getting along.

Asked if he ever expected to see the sergeant again, Young said, "He can come to my home any time he wants to. The folks down there might think it's funny, but he saved my life. He's as good a man as I am."

These incidents are threads in the pattern of the military achievement, a racial about-face unparalleled by any similar development in modern history. It has taken place within a decade, without bloodshed and virtually unnoticed.

A dozen years ago segregation of Negroes was the rule in virtually all branches of the service. Most military leaders expected — many wanted — it to stay that way for a long time to come.

Yet in 1953 segregation had been officially discarded, and integration of all servicemen, of whatever race or nationality, was the firm policy of every branch of the military service.

The racial barrier had been virtually wiped out in the Air Force, and in the Navy outside the almost entirely Negro Steward's Branch. The Army was far along the road to elimination of its all-Negro units, both at home and abroad. Negro marines trained side by side with white marines on the Carolina beaches, fought alongside them in Korea; there were no longer any all-Negro marine units.

There had not yet been a total transformation of long-established patterns of racial thinking and acting; it would be years, perhaps generations, before Negroes found absolute acceptance throughout the military world, before it would be common to hear of Negro generals and admirals. There would yet be many skirmishes, large and small, as old patterns of inequality lingered on or sought to reassert themselves, and champions of the new order joined battle. But the road was open and there could be no turning back.

The new policy had been tried in the fire of battle in Korea and officially was recorded a success. Leading officials of all services who had seen it work said almost unanimously, "We will never go back to segregation."

Gone were complaints of wide-scale "melting away" of Negro units that plagued many American commanders in two world wars and during the early months of the Korean War. Exhaustive studies rated America's Negro soldiers on close par with white fighting men *when serving in racially mixed units*.

Far from the general predictions of ruined efficiency, wrecked morale, even bloody revolt, white units showed little reaction when Negroes were sprinkled among their ranks. Some officers even reported *heightened morale* among their once all-white units after Negroes were added.

Detailed official analyses, backed by statements of hundreds of field commanders, showed that racial conflict — once a critical military problem that led to repeated bloody riots — had all but vanished. With Negroes and whites no longer grouped separately, there was apparently little motive for racial "gang" conflict.

This about-face on race had far-reaching implications for the future, not only in the military realm but in America's total race pattern and its relations with the rest of the world.

On the military front, according to Army technical advisers, it meant that the nation's big reservoir of Negro manpower could be counted on to swell the ranks of an effective, up-to-date fighting machine in event of a major emergency, manpower that would not be sullen, bitter and of doubtful reliability as had happened too often in the past.

For the nation as a whole, the military was spearheading an accelerated shift away from the long-standing pattern of racial segregation throughout the United States. Negroes and whites in the armed forces were not just training and fighting together; they were eating at the same tables, sleeping next to one another and drinking beer together at military post canteens. They were going to church and the movies together, often attending the same dances.

Families of Negro and white servicemen were coming more and more to live next to one another on military reservations. Their wives gossiped over the clothesline and learned to be friendly neighbors. Their children attended schools together on military posts. There were already several unsegregated schools at bases in the South, though segregated schools were still the rule in nearby communities.

This tide of integration was inexorably seeping into the civilian world, where similar currents were at work. Files in the Pentagon reported that white families invited Negro servicemen home to dinner or for a week-end, in the South as well as the North. Restaurants near military posts decided to admit Negroes along with white soldiers. Negroes and white soldiers sat side by side on a city bus in Columbia, South Carolina, where this was against the law.

A white industrialist marveled at a Negro engineer's ability to repair a breakdown in equipment that baffled his white engineers. He found that the Negro had learned how in the Navy.

These were but a few signposts on a road whose end could still be but dimly envisioned. Civilians seeking to accelerate progress down that road might learn important lessons from the military.

"In civilian life they [Negroes] are bunched," said a hardboiled southern general. "They've got to be unbunched."

The racial shift in the U.S. armed forces also appeared certain to have a significant effect on this country's international relations, and perhaps — in the long run — on the course of history. Russian propaganda in recent years had been stepping up the race-hate theme. One of its most insidious efforts was to try to convince the world's darker races that the West — principally the United States — sought literally to exterminate dark-skinned peoples. According to U.S. State Department experts, nearly half of recent Russian propaganda had been concentrated on race, linking Communist germ warfare charges with alleged racial brutality in this country. This had aroused anew a dormant fear that another war might develop into a racial conflict, with the world's darker peoples arrayed against white men.

The actual facts of what official America was doing, when widely known, could be expected to give Russia's race propaganda a major setback. And it was bound to become known with U.S. forces, Negro and white visibly intermingled, stationed in nearly fifty countries on six continents.

Racial integration in the U.S. armed forces already had begun to remove doubts among America's allies, many of whom long looked suspiciously on U.S. pronouncements about freedom and equality while American Negroes suffered grave discrimination in all walks of life.

It might eventually have some effect on racial patterns in other countries. Some American officials even considered ways of showing the South Africans, caught in the throes of bitter racial struggle, the success of the U.S. military racial accomplishment.

The story of how the color barrier was breached by the military is one of the most dramatic success stories in modern American history, doubly so because it has been on so vast a scale. Changing times and attitudes played a part: the increasing education of Negroes, who have been moving steadily closer to whites in skill and training, including the ability to handle weapons of modern warfare; the growing belief among American whites of the essential equality of races; the readiness of both races to learn to get along together.

It is also a story of men of courage and foresight who were able to see that military efficiency and democratic ideals could go hand in hand: men like the late President Franklin D. Roosevelt, who pushed and prodded the services into allowing greater opportunities for Negroes during World War II; James V.

Forrestal, a Wall Street financier who felt, as Secretary of the Navy, that America's future demanded recognition of the equality of all men; Stuart Symington, who refused to recognize racial distinctions and used high-powered business methods to bring racial equality to the Air Force; Christopher Sargent, a minister's son who, as a mere navy lieutenant, helped to inspire one of the greatest experiments the Navy ever undertook; Lieutenant General Anthony C. McAuliffe, an Army commander who had the guts not only to defy German armored might but also to change his mind and defy tradition; Harry S. Truman, a stubborn man from Missouri who insisted on taking literally the Bible and the Constitution when they spoke of equality and brotherhood; of many others, inside and outside the military services, who led, or inspired, or helped, or went willingly along, with the new tide of racial change.

It is also a story of bitter resistance, tradition-crusted "brass and braid," some of whom had to be retired to make room for new ways, of stubborn politicians who would not see that old methods had outlived their usefulness.

Perhaps, most of all, it is the story of the coming of age of the American Negro; of Negroes who battled through nearly two centuries for the "right to fight" for their country; of Negro men and women who, despite grave abuse, generally kept their sense of national loyalty and dignity and, when the white ranks of the military parted to receive them, marched in and took their places — proudly, and for the most part quietly.

TWO

"Thoroughly Unreliable"

In March, 1945, Truman Gibson, Negro Civilian Aide to Secretary of War Henry L. Stimson, aroused anger and indignation among certain American Negroes by telling a press conference in Rome, Italy, that the all-Negro 92nd U.S. Division had been subject to "panicky" retreats and "melting away" of some individual soldiers. The conference was called in response to questions from correspondents about reported bad performance in the 92nd. Mr. Gibson, knowing the facts, evidently felt it wise to tell the press what had happened and to add certain background information which never got printed.[1]

---

[1] Mr. Gibson was asked about his statement during the preparation of this book. He wrote as follows: "I at no time said that units of the 92nd Division "melted away." I did confirm the fact well known to all news-

11

12

This report, coming from a Negro and therefore assumed to be unprejudiced, was taken by many whites as proof of the inferiority of Negro troops in combat.

Gibson went on to say that the record of the division "does not prove that Negroes can't fight; there is no question in my mind about the courage of Negro officers or soldiers." He attributed failures of the division chiefly to high illiteracy and lack of sufficient training. But his unfavorable statements received greater attention than his explanations in American newspapers and among most military men.

Behind the report was a series of long and bitter events involving the Negro 92nd Division, and a confused picture of Negro troops in earlier wars. Ahead of it lay more confusion and dissatisfaction with all-Negro fighting units, and a solution that was to shed the cold light of hindsight on the mistakes of the past.

An official Army War College account, prepared by Major Paul Goodman, a member of the staff and faculty, related how a task force of the 92nd Division, dug in on the

---

papermen in the Theater including Negro war correspondents, that individuals in some units had retreated in a panicky fashion. I pointed out in the press conference and subsequently in the War Department that segregation as a policy would inevitably produce militarily unsound results. In the conference I contrasted the learning level of the enlisted personnel of the 92nd Division with that existing in white divisions. I pointed out that the Army applied one standard to white units and quite another to those comprised of Negro troops.

"I further pointed out that military authorities repeatedly stated that no units could efficiently operate which consisted of more than 10 percent class 5 men. The 92nd Division included more than 80 percent class 5 troops. The investigation further revealed and I therefore stated that because only Negro replacements could be furnished the 92nd Division, untrained service troops had been rushed into combat while trained infantry replacements were made available to white units."

south side of the Cinquale Canal in Italy, was alerted on the night of February 7, 1945, for an attack on the German Gothic Line. Allied forces had driven northward from Rome and were preparing to push the stubbornly resisting Nazis into the mountains as a prelude to the windup of the Italian campaign. The Germans were heavily entrenched in the Apuan Alps, their guns commanding the flat coastal area around the Cinquale, a small canal meandering through farm and resort country near Forte dei Marmi.

It was the first big attack of the war for the all-Negro "Buffalo" Division, inactivated after World War I and resurrected in World War II, when the Army became swamped with draftees and Negro groups clamored for the right of Negroes to enter combat service. Officers had put their men through an elaborate dress rehearsal three days earlier.

The American artillery opened up at 4:30 A.M. on February 8. What followed was a highly controversial chapter in American military history. The War College account told how the first attack wave moved out at 5 A.M. in the pre-dawn cold, the tanks rumbling across the canal and engineers leaping off to remove mines from the beach. Then one of the leading tanks broke down. Another, trying to pass, drowned its motor in the canal. By this time the German coastal guns at Punta Bianca had found the range and begun pumping shells into the advancing troops. One landed in the midst of the ten-man command group, killing seven white officers.

The task force commander, Lieutenant Colonel Edward L. Rowny, miraculously unhurt, rushed forward, expecting to find his men pushing ahead toward the foremost tanks which were rumbling slowly toward the German positions. Instead he said he found the Negro infantrymen frantically digging in under the stalled tanks along the beach.

He said he ordered them to advance but "they did not move but kept digging further and further into their holes beside the tanks." A Negro tank sergeant suggested removing some of the dead sprawled along the canal bank and he and Rowny hauled bodies behind trees. Then, said Rowny, he and the sergeant "escorted little groups forward toward the most forward tanks."

The cut-up task force managed to hold a thin line across the canal until nightfall. In the morning Rowny said he looked around and found only a handful of men left; "the others had drifted to the rear."

During three days of heavy shelling and German counterattacks, Rowny tried to hold his men in their tenuous foothold. The War College study reported, however, that "straggling was excessive and disorganization evident in nearly every unit across the division front."

Major General Edward M. Almond, Virginia-born division commander, ordered the attack ended on February 11.

"We pulled them out," said a senior division officer later. "They were thoroughly unreliable."

An independent study of the 92nd Division, made after the war by Miss Jean Byers, who was given access to War Department records, put a different light on the battle of the Cinquale Canal. It stated that the beaches along which the attack was made were mined, and untenable because all surrounding high ground was in the hands of the Germans. It quoted a white officer of the division as saying that the attack "seemed to most junior officers to be poorly planned by the division commander and staff," being a simultaneous attack by three regiments on a wide, well-defended front with "no attempt to concentrate our strength at any point of suspected enemy weakness," and "practically no deception or surprise."

Miss Byers cited reports that many of the division's senior

officers were southern whites with "conventional southern attitudes" toward Negroes, and that "the majority of the (white)
officers believed that the experiment of using Negroes in combat would fail." (Rowny denied, in correspondence with this
author, that either southern officers predominated or that the
division's officers lacked faith in the fighting ability of Negroes.)

Miss Byers also noted the record of individual bravery among
Negroes of the division, two of whom won Distinguished Service Crosses in Italy, one a Distinguished Service Medal, six-
teen Legion of Merit Medals, ninety-five Silver Stars and 723
Bronze Stars.

Miss Byers did not minimize the combat failures of the
division; and both her study and that of the War College noted
that more than 90 percent of the men, mostly draftees from the
South with little schooling, fell into the two lowest Army mental test groups — a factor which many Army officials then
believed made it literally impossible to train and organize a
successful combat corps. Rowny himself told this author later
that he did not think a white outfit operating under a similar
handicap could have done better.

Military analysts might someday arrive at a final evaluation
of the combat service of the 92nd Division. But the most
significant aspect of the controversy was what it led to.

Not long after the abortive Cinquale Canal attack, a council
was held at Major General Almond's headquarters at Viareggio.
Present were General George C. Marshall, Army Chief of Staff;
Lieutenant General Mark W. Clark, commander of the Fif-
teenth Army Group; Lieutenant General Lucien D. Truscott,
commander of the Fifth Army; and Major General Willis D.
Crittenberger, head of the Fourth Corps.

Almond told of his months of frustration with the Negro

soldiers. Under other circumstances, regardless of the underlying causes, the entire division would have been pulled out. But a spring offensive was under preparation and all available organized troops were needed.

Marshall, according to the War College narrative, proposed the solution that was adopted. The best elements of two of the division's three Negro regiments were consolidated into the third regiment, the 370th. The remainder of the other two Negro regiments were sent to the rear and replaced by two others: the 473rd Infantry Regiment, battle-hardened white veterans of Tunisia, Salerno and Cassino; and the 442nd Infantry Regiment, the Japanese-American fighting team that had already won battle honors in southern France.

On April 5, 1945, at 5 A.M., the reconstituted Negro 370th Regiment and the Nisei began a side-by-side attack aimed at Massa, German stronghold in the mountains, a target of the abortive February thrust. The Nisei, recounted a division staff officer later, pushed five miles through the mountains in one day and the Germans, "who didn't know we didn't have all Negroes any more, didn't know what hit them." The Negro regiment, he added, "went 1,000 yards in two days."

Many factors could be discussed in connection with this action — the differing terrain confronting the Negro and Nisei units; the fact that the Nisei regiment boasted the highest individual mental test scores of any infantry unit in the U.S. Army, compared to the Negro division, which had the lowest; the greater motivation of the Japanese-Americans, who were fighting hopefully to erase the shadow cast on their loyalty by the Japanese attack on Pearl Harbor, while the Negroes had come from segregation, had trained and fought in segregation, and knew they would return to second-class citizenship when the war was over.

General Marshall said later that elements of the 92nd Division other than the infantry — artillery, engineers, etc.— "so far as I know gave a good account of themselves." But Almond's disappointment with Negroes of his command, etched unforgettably by the Cinquale Canal and other setbacks, echoed in the ears of military planners long after the war was over; the other side of the story often forgotten.

The prevailing military belief that Negroes were useless in war except for labor duties had a long, and often distorted, historical background, and died hard among military planners.

Negro troops had handled tough assignments throughout America's military history and won fame in several engagements, such as the Battle of San Juan Hill in Cuba in the Spanish-American War. But many military leaders remained convinced after World War II that Negroes were unreliable fighters.

They recalled how the 368th Infantry Regiment of the original all-Negro 92nd Division had become utterly demoralized in an attack in the Argonne during World War I. The reasons, such as inadequate training, inferior officers and lack of fire power, were forgotten.

Major General Robert Lee Bullard, World War I commander of the Second Army, which included the 92nd Division, said in his memoirs that Negroes were emotionally unsuited for war: they were "lazy, slothful, superstitious, imaginative . . . if you need combat soldiers, and especially if you need them in a hurry, don't put your time upon Negroes."

Army planners in the Pentagon, meeting after World War II to look ahead, took tentative steps toward a new method of handling Negro soldiers, but timidly, avoiding any clear-cut decision on the basic problem of segregation. The Navy meanwhile, faced with similar trouble with all-Negro units, had quietly altered its racial policies in favor of non-segregation, and the newly independent Air Force soon followed the same course, moving even faster than the Navy.

On June 25, 1950, North Korean armies, heavily supplied by Russia, crossed the 38th parallel in Korea in a lightning attack and began pushing the stunned Korean Republic forces toward the sea. The United States rushed to the aid of South Korea, sweeping nearly a score of United Nations into the conflict.

While the Communist southward tide was still running strong, the all-Negro 24th Infantry Regiment took Yech'on — the first town recaptured by American forces, though but a brief halt in the Allied withdrawal toward Pusan. But before long, into the headquarters of Lieutenant General Walton H. Walker, Major General William F. Dean, General Douglas MacArthur and the Pentagon, came familiar stories.

All-Negro units again were proving "unreliable." In attacks, particularly at night, Negroes would get close to the enemy, then "bug out"—melt into the night, to turn up the next day insisting they were lost.

Harry A. Martin, writing in the *Saturday Evening Post* for June 16, 1951, reported that Lieutenant Colonel Melvin Russell Blair, commander of the 3rd Battalion of the 24th Regiment, "fled through the wintry dark in his drawers" one night to escape capture by encircling Chinese Red forces who had put his Negro guard to flight without firing a shot. Reaching the safety of another unit at dawn, he was said to have watched the three companies of his battalion cut to pieces, most of the men fleeing "like rabbits" when the Chinese came at them.

Driving down the road seeking the remnants of his force, Blair said he heard singing with a bounce he liked. Calling to a group of Negroes huddled around a fire in the snow, he asked what the song was.

"Sir," he quoted a soldier as replying, "this is the official song of the 24th Infantry Regiment. This is the Bug Out Boogie." He said the soldier sang him the words:

> *"When them Chinese mortars begins to thud,*
> *"The old Deuce-Four begin to bug...."*

Colonel John T. Corley, commander of the 24th Regiment, said later in an interview for a Negro newspaper that although the record of the regiment was "spotty," with good as well as bad pages, the men fled on the night in question because they had been fighting five days and were "dead on their feet." He doubted the "Bug Out Boogie" incident.[1]

But Blair's account was given wide circulation. A few weeks later Blair himself was back at the Pentagon where his hair-raising stories had a ready audience.

By then, however, a totally new solution to the historic dilemma of Negro troops was in the making. Soon the bleak hills and watery rice fields of Korea became the ultimate proving ground for one of the most significant racial developments in United States history.

[1] Published in the Pittsburgh *Courier* in three installments, June 23 and 30 and July 7, 1951.

THREE

In Time of Need

Since the first slaves were brought to Jamestown, Virginia, in 1619, Negro soldiers and sailors had fought in all America's wars, though until today the wisdom of their employment and quality of their combat performance had been repeatedly questioned.

Crispus Attucks, a runaway Massachusetts slave, was the first person shot and one of the five slain in the Boston Massacre of March 5, 1770, that helped spark the Revolutionary War. His body was laid in a common grave along with the white citizens who died that day. At Bunker Hill another ex-slave, Peter Salem, was credited with killing British Major Pitcairn, whose order to fire on the Minutemen at Lexington officially began the American Revolution.

Although free Negroes and a few slaves were in the Continental forces from the start, General George Washington ordered their enlistment halted on November 12, 1775. Some patriot leaders considered Negroes savages and not fit to fight the battles of free men. But after the British offered slaves their freedom to join the Loyalist troops, Washington reversed himself and authorized recruiters to accept free Negroes. Congress approved the new policy despite many objections.

Slaves later were officially taken into the Continental ranks when Washington was hard-pressed for men. The Rhode Island legislature authorized enlistment of one regiment of slaves, who were given their freedom, and their masters remunerated up to 120 English pounds per man. Most of the 629 slaves in New Hampshire gained their freedom the same way. Before the war was over Negroes were serving in the armies of all thirteen colonies — as well as on the British side — and in the Continental Navy. An estimated 3,000 to 5,000 served with the Colonial armies at one time or another.

Thus far there has been no thorough evaluation of Negro troops in the Revolutionary War. Most available sources speak favorably of them, but an Army War College study in 1942 said there were not enough facts to evaluate their combat record. Arnold's *History of Rhode Island* said that the Rhode Island Negro regiment, under Colonel Greene, "distinguished itself by deeds of desperate valor" and "three times drove back the Hessians, who charged repeatedly down the hill to dislodge them."

But in February, 1782, Lieutenant Colonel Olney, in Rhode Island to obtain men for the Colonial Army, issued orders not to enlist "Indians, negroes and mulattoes," whom he said "long and fatal experience" had shown "do not (and from a total want of Perseverance and Fortitude to bear the various Fatigues incident to the Army cannot) answer the public service. . . ."

The Revolution launched the sharp conflict over Negro soldiers in America that has lasted up to the present. The South Carolina legislature, refusing to arm Negroes though a few served unofficially in the colony's ranks, said, ". . . republican pride . . . disdains to commit the defense of the country to servile bands" or to share arms "with a color to which the idea of inferiority is inseparably connected."

Henry Laurens, a South Carolinian who urged the enlistment of slaves, said he was opposed by "a triple-headed monster that shed the baneful influence of avarice, prejudice and pusillanimity in all our assemblies."

Differing views of the value of Negro fighting men continued in the War of 1812. Commodore Oliver H. Perry called a group of replacements sent him "a motley set — blacks, soldiers, boys," but said he was glad to get "anything in the shape of a man." Commodore Isaac Chauncey, his superior, replied he had "yet to learn that the color of the skin, or the cut and trimmings of the coat, can affect a man's qualifications or usefulness."

In the land phase of the war, General Andrew Jackson appealed to the free Negroes of New Orleans to defend the city against the threatening British. In a letter to Governor Claiborne of Louisiana, he said that the Negroes must be "either for us or against us: mistrust them and you make them your enemies; place confidence in them and you engage them by every dear and honorable tie to the interest of the country."

More than 600 Negroes, all men of property, volunteered. Jackson praised their "great bravery" after New Orleans was saved from the British.

By the Civil War, slavery had disappeared in the North and become a fixture in the South. Lincoln and his cabinet had no idea of enrolling Negroes at the start of the war, and volunteers were turned away. A group of New York Negroes rented a hall and began drilling; on the advice of the Chief of Police, who feared riots, they disbanded.

Prevailing sentiment in the Lincoln cabinet at first was that slavery was not to be interfered with, that the war was a rebellion and would be put down in three months. But as the fighting wore on, and the North needed men, the view changed. Despite bitter opposition of white soldiers from large cities and border states, Congress passed a law on July 17, 1862, authorizing enlistment of slaves of rebel owners — chiefly for labor duties.

In January, 1863, after the Emancipation Proclamation was promulgated, formal recruiting of Negroes in the North and South was authorized. Frederick Douglass, famed Negro anti-slavery journalist, appealed: "Men of Color, to Arms! . . . This is our golden opportunity. Let us accept it and forever wipe out the dark reproaches unsparingly hurled against us by our enemies."

The first recorded Civil War battle in which Negro troops fought as a unit was at Island Mounds, Missouri, on October 28, 1862. The First Kansas Colored Volunteers, enlisted without specific authority, defeated Cockerel's superior Confederate force. Thereafter Negro troops fought in many engagements, but most were put to work on fortifications, railroads, keeping open the Mississippi River, guarding plantations and doing plantation work. White officers in charge of Negroes, as well as Negroes themselves, protested — usually in vain — against being deprived of the chance for combat. An estimated 200,000 Negroes served as soldiers in the Union Army, and another 200,000 as civilian laborers with the Army.

The Confederacy, bitter about northern enlistment of ex-slaves, did not seek to arm Negroes until early 1865, too late to be of any material aid. General J. B. Hood of the Confederate Army, in his book *Advance and Retreat,* wrote later that early freeing of the slaves and their enlistment by the South "would, in my opinion, have given us our independence."

One Confederate unit, the 49th Georgia Regiment, even suggested a Civil War equivalent of modern-day "integration." Officers of the regiment, with their men "almost unanimously" approving, proposed on March 15, 1865, that Negroes from Georgia be conscripted to fill vacancies in their ranks, apparently to serve side by side with their white fellow-Georgians.

The officers argued, "When in former years, for pecuniary purposes, we did not consider it disgraceful to labor with negroes in the field or at the same workbench, we certainly will not look upon it in any other light at this time, when an end so glorious as our independence is to be achieved." They said it would, among other things, ". . . cement a reciprocal attachment between the men now in service and the negroes highly beneficial to the service . . . ."

The plan was endorsed by officers all the way up the line through Major General H. Heth, commander of the Third Corps of the Army of Northern Virginia. But it was rejected by General Robert E. Lee, who commended the regiment's "spirit" and proposed instead the formation of separate companies of Negro troops. By then, however, the Civil War was about over and nothing came of the South's belated attempt to arm its slaves.

Though there were adverse reports of the fighting of Negroes in the Civil War, officers who commanded them were mostly favorable. General Ulysses S. Grant praised raw Negro recruits under him at Vicksburg, asserting, "All that have been tried fought bravely." However, Professor Bell I. Wiley recorded in his history, *Southern Negroes,* that "the almost universal testimony of those in position to observe . . . is that they (the Negroes) ran when their charge on the crest (at Petersburg, Virginia, in 1865) was repulsed. Their commander, General Ferrero, testified before the committee investigating the battle that they 'retreated in great disorder and confusion.'"

Wiley summed up that, "While the colored soldiers were not as efficient fighters as their northern eulogists represented them, it is just as true that they were not the inconsequential cowards depicted by their southern disparagers."

After the Civil War, the Federal Army was reorganized. Congress provided for four permanent Negro regiments, which became the 9th and 10th Cavalry, organized in 1866, and the 24th and 25th Infantry, organized respectively in 1868 and 1869. With few exceptions they were staffed by white officers, many of whom, like General John J. Pershing, later became famous.

Perhaps the best-known Negro officer in these regiments was Benjamin O. Davis, who enlisted with the 9th Cavalry in July, 1899, and was the first Negro in United States history to become a general.

The 9th and 10th Cavalry fought Indians in the western push of America's frontiers. The Indians, who called the Negroes "buffalo soldiers," possibly because of the buffalo hide coats they wore in winter, reputedly considered it bad medicine to scalp them. This may have been due partly to their short, wiry hair which was hard to seize.

The four Negro regiments fought alongside white regiments at the Battle of San Juan Hill in Cuba that preceded land victory in the Spanish-American War in 1898. Pershing, then a lieutenant with the 10th Cavalry, said that at Las Guasimas, before San Juan Hill, the 10th charged up the hill, "opened a disastrous enfilading fire upon the Spanish right, thus relieving" Theodore Roosevelt's pinned-down Rough Riders. The correspondent of the *Washington Post* cabled his paper that "if it had not been for the Negro cavalry, the Rough Riders would have been exterminated."[1]

The 24th Regiment was ordered to Siboney, Cuba, for guard duty after the Spanish surrender. Its members volunteered almost to a man to nurse yellow fever patients filling the hospitals there. When the men serving as nurses came down with fever, their places were quickly filled by fresh volunteers. Although the Negroes then were known colloquially as "Immunes," because of their supposed immunity to fever, only twenty-four of the 456 men who marched to Siboney escaped yellow fever, and many died.

By the time of World War I, racial tensions in the nation had become more acute. There was widespread bitterness toward Negro troops.

On August 13, 1906, nine to twenty Negro soldiers left Fort Brown, near Brownsville, Texas, and rode into town, shooting as they came. They fired into houses where people lay sleeping, killed a bartender, wounded a policeman and shot at everything they saw moving.

Many eyewitnesses said the soldiers were Negroes of the 25th Infantry Regiment, who had become infuriated when their passes to town were canceled the previous day after a scuffle between a Negro soldier and a white citizen. There had been bad relations between the regiment and the town for months.

During a two-year investigation, men of the 25th steadfastly refused to admit any knowledge of the shooting or the perpetrators. President Theodore Roosevelt at last ordered three en-

---

[1] Cited in A *Study of the Negro in Military Service* by Jean Byers.

tire companies of the regiment dishonorably discharged. A Senate investigation upheld the President in 1908.

The memory of Brownsville had not died in the South when Negroes of the 24th Regiment at Houston, Texas, embittered by goading and insults from the citizens, shot up the city in mid-August, 1917, killing seventeen white persons and wounding more than a score of others. With what has been called a "slight pretense of a trial," thirteen of the Negroes who "seemed to be implicated" were hanged for murder and mutiny and forty-one sentenced to life imprisonment.

Anger against Negro troops in the South blazed after Houston. Mayor Floyd of Spartanburg, South Carolina, protested plans to send the New York 15th National Guard Negro Regiment to nearby Camp Wadsworth, saying, "This thing is like waving a red flag in the face of a bull."

But Colonel William Hayward, an active Republican and son of Senator Monroe L. Hayward of Nebraska, had organized the regiment as a challenge to prove Negroes could fight. On arriving at Camp Wadsworth, he stood on a bathhouse roof and told his men this was their chance to show the people of Spartanburg and the world what educated Negroes were like. He begged them not to return violence even if it were used against them.

One evening Noble Sissle, Negro drum major in the regiment band, went into a hotel to buy a newspaper. On the way out he was kicked onto his face and cursed by the proprietor. White soldiers in the hotel started to rush the proprietor, but were suddenly snapped to attention and marched onto the street — by Lieutenant James Europe, leader of the band, a full-blooded Negro who had watched from the sidewalk.

Negroes of the regiment, heeding their colonel's plea, took other insults and beatings from the townspeople without returning violence. But Brigadier General Charles L. Phillips, commander at Camp Wadsworth, decided the regiment should be moved in fairness to the men and to avoid a threatening explosion in the town. On New Year's Day, 1918, it landed in France, among the first American troops to touch French soil.

Promptly on arrival the men were put at pick and shovel work by the general in command at St. Nazaire, a sharp disappointment after they had been trained for combat. Hayward finally persuaded Pershing to give them front-line combat duty.

Renamed the 369th Infantry Regiment and sent to serve directly under the French, this unit was called by Hayward "Les Enfants Perdus" ("The Lost Children"). Of them he said, "Our great American general simply put the black orphan in a basket, set it on the doorstep of the French, pulled the bell and went away." He said that a French colonel to whom he told this replied, "Weelcome, leetle black babbie."

Hayward, in an official report to the War Department after the war, said his men got along well with the French poilus and officers, despite language difficulties. Under French command, he said, they never lost a prisoner, a trench or a foot of ground during 191 days under fire, longer than any other American unit. They were believed to be the first United States troops to reach the Rhine.

One of the exploits of the 369th was headlined as "The Battle of Henry Johnson" by the old *New York World*. Johnson, a little ex-redcap from the New York Central railroad station at Albany, New York, one night beat off a German raiding party of about twenty men who tried to capture his patrol partner, Private Needham Roberts of Trenton, New Jersey, at a front-line outpost. The wounded Roberts, unable to rise, hurled grenades at the Germans, while Johnson swung his rifle and slashed with his bolo knife to such effect that the raiders were routed, leaving four dead behind.

Johnson and Roberts were both awarded the Croix de Guerre for their feat, the first American soldiers to win the French medal in World War I. Later their entire regiment was granted the Croix de Guerre unit citation, as were two of the three other Negro regiments of the 93rd Division, a division that served directly under the French. Hayward, who left the United States with bitterness because his regiment was not allowed to cross the Atlantic with the Rainbow Division — he was told black was not one of the colors of the rainbow — led his men in a triumphant parade up New York's Fifth Avenue after the Armistice.

But World War I stood out in the minds of most military men as a sorry memory as far as Negro troops were concerned. Much of this centered around the all-Negro 92nd Division, which fought under American command and got most of the attention. Controversy over the 92nd in that war fills volumes. Essential facts are that it was poorly trained, its few Negro officers were far below the level of white officers in education and training, and elements of one of its regiments — the 368th — became demoralized and fled to the rear during five days of the Meuse-Argonne offensive beginning September 26, 1918.

After a War Department investigation later, Secretary of War Newton D. Baker, defending the Negroes' record, said the circumstances "do not justify many of the highly colored accounts which have been given of the behavior of the troops in this action, and they afford no basis at all for any of the general assumptions with regard to the action of colored troops in this battle and elsewhere in France."

But though there were many reports of creditable fighting by Negro units, and many individual awards for bravery, an

Army War College study in 1942 declared that "contemporary comment by responsible officers" about both all-Negro divisions — the 92nd and 93rd — was "mostly unfavorable. . . ."

There was an even darker side to the World War I story for Negroes. Emmett J. Scott, a Negro, former secretary to Booker T. Washington and retained during the war as Special Assistant to Baker to handle racial problems, wrote afterward of wretched conditions in Negro training camps in the United States. He recorded organized efforts to humiliate Negro officers, and cited an order from Brigadier General James B. Erwin, who commanded the 92nd Division after the Armistice, that Negroes of the division were not to speak to French women. Military police arrested Negroes caught talking to women in French towns.

Scott reported that a document was issued "from Pershing's headquarters" on August 7, 1918, asking French officers not to permit "familiarity and indulgence" toward American Negro officers; not to eat with them, shake hands with them or talk to them beyond military necessity. It referred to Negroes, said Scott, as a "menace of degeneracy which had to be prevented by the gulf . . . between the two races . . . ." There was no available evidence, however, that Pershing, who objected to discrimination against Negroes, was personally responsible for the order.

Thousands of Negroes who had been drilled for combat were put in labor battalions in France, in keeping with the views of many American officers that they were fit only for manual work. Of about 140,000 Negro troops sent to France, roughly 40,000 saw combat. Conditions in the labor camps, reported Scott, were often deplorable, with sickness rampant.

Representative William L. Dawson, Negro congressman from Illinois who served with the 92nd Division in World War I, said Negroes received such brutal treatment in some military hospitals that when he was clubbed by a German rifle, he refused to go to the hospital for "mistreatment," getting his men to tape up his wound and bearing a lame shoulder for life as a consequence. A Negro officer recalled that Red Cross girls, carrying hot chocolate and coffee for the men, turned back when they saw Negro soldiers.

Dawson said later, that if another war came, he would go to jail for counseling Negroes to stay out should the same conditions prevail. He changed his mind when World War II came because of what he considered the greater menace of Nazism.

He lived to see a new day for Negroes in the nation's armed forces.

FOUR

Cracks in the Wall

A report by a committee at the Army War College in the 1939-40 school year said the Negro was "far below the white in capacity to absorb instruction," and gave the following story to illustrate its view on the value of Negro officers.

A staff officer stopped at a crossroad and asked a Negro sentry which way one road went.

"I don't know, sir."

"Where does that road go?"

"I don't know, sir."

"Well, what are you here for?"

"I don't know, sir."

"Who put you here?"

"The Captain, sir."

"Where is the Captain?"

"The Captain? He's right over here, sir, but he won't help you none. He's a nigger too!"

That blunt but outspoken report typified the general attitude toward Negroes that prevailed among military leaders between World Wars I and II.

American Negro troops in France were rushed home after World War I — to avoid trouble, the French were told. When France's Marshal Foch objected to letting any American division leave before the peace treaty was signed, Major General Bullard, according to *The Colored Soldier in the U.S. Army,* a War College study, sent word to Foch that he could not be responsible for what the Negroes might do to French women if allowed to remain.

There were, indeed, triumphant parades. Arthur W. Little, in his book, *From Harlem to the Rhine,* told of the roaring welcome given to Colonel Hayward's "Enfants Perdus" as they paraded up Fifth Avenue between "Welcome Home Our Heroes" posters. Harlem went wild over the black doughboys, including the wounded Henry Johnson, who was hauled along in an open touring car.

But in the South it was different. Returning Negro soldiers were ordered off trains and busses, forced to strip off their uniforms and medals. John Hope Franklin's *From Slavery to Freedom* lists more than seventy Negroes lynched in the first year after the war, including ten soldiers still in uniform, and fourteen Negroes burned publicly, eleven of them alive. There were twenty-five race riots between June and December, and Negroes were forced out of jobs by returning white soldiers.

In a rash of War College studies between wars, nearly all calling for continued segregation, a few officers proposed blending Negroes in white units. A far-seeing infantry colonel,

James K. Parsons, said individual Negroes should be assigned in a ratio of about 2,000 to a division, 300 to a regiment, thirty to a rifle company and one to a squad. He said this would reduce racial antagonism to a minimum and permit a steady quality in army units. His prophetic view was repeated almost verbatim in 1952 by a tough southern general, describing to this writer what the Army was then doing with Negro soldiers.

But the Army's plans for Negro troops showed "no forward thinking in practical terms" between world wars, in the judgment of a high-level board of officers sitting in review after World War II. A War Department letter of July 12, 1923, provided for use of Negroes in an emergency on a limited scale. It specified "No Negro troops are to be mobilized in the State of Texas."

This policy was modified in 1938 to provide for enlistment of Negroes in the same proportion as Negroes to the general population — then about 9 percent. In event of war, Negroes were to be used in approximately the same ratio as whites in combat and non-combat arms "unless conditions" required otherwise. Segregation was to be continued. No Negro officers were to be placed in command of white officers or men.

But after Hitler invaded Poland "conditions" played hob with the Army's carefully laid plans. For one thing, Negro leaders, many of whom had preached "close ranks" and win the war in World War I, now were urging Negroes to demand equal treatment in the armed forces. Walter White, Executive Secretary of the National Association for the Advancement of Colored People, said in his autobiography, *A Man Called White,* that at one point President Roosevelt told him pressure was being brought on the President and the Justice Department to prosecute the more virulent Negro editors for sedition.

Though nothing came of this, the growing Negro protests,

combined with the current political situation and the presence of Franklin Roosevelt — and Eleanor Roosevelt — in the White House, led to a series of far-reaching developments.

On September 14, 1940, President Roosevelt signed the Selective Service Act, which contained a clause barring racial discrimination toward men drafted into the armed forces. This was inserted in the bill by Representative Hamilton Fish, New York Republican who had been an officer of Hayward's World War I Negro regiment. Fish, known as a friend of Negro soldiers, was quickly persuaded to put through the non-discrimination clause by a committee on Participation of Negroes in the War, set up by the Pittsburgh *Courier,* prominent Negro newspaper.

The committee was "sure" the language of the amendment, which its members had drafted with great care, would abolish segregation in the armed forces. To their bitter disappointment, it failed of this goal. But it had a powerful impact, particularly on the Navy, through forcing it later to take in large numbers of Negroes, for whom billets had to be found.

But Negro leaders did not rest with the draft amendment. On September 27, 1940, with a crucial election approaching, Mr. Roosevelt received a delegation of three Negroes, Walter White, A. Philip Randolph of the Brotherhood of Sleeping Car Porters and T. Arnold Hill, acting secretary of the National Urban League.

As related by White in his autobiography, they urged the President to end segregation in the military at once; he promised to see what he could do. When he asked the Army for its recommendations, Assistant Secretary of War Robert P. Patterson sent him a memo, approved by Secretary of War Henry L. Stimson and General George C. Marshall, Chief of Staff, stating that the War Department policy of segregation must be maintained. It "has been proven satisfactory over a long period of years and to make changes would produce situations destructive to morale and detrimental to the preparations for national defense," the memo declared.[1]

The memo was initialed by FDR on October 8, 1940, and made public by his press secretary, Steve Early, the following day, together with the implication — according to White — that the Negro delegation had approved it. This they angrily denied.

Shortly afterward Early kicked a New York Negro policeman in the groin for refusing to let him cross a police line guarding the President.

The Republicans seized on these incidents to woo the Negro vote, and alarmed friends of FDR asked White what could be done. He replied that the only possible step would be to end discrimination in the armed forces and in industry.

On October 16 the White House announced that William H. Hastie, Negro dean of the Howard University Law School, had been appointed Civilian Aide to Stimson; that Colonel Benjamin 0. Davis had been promoted to brigadier general, the first Negro to become a general; and that Colonel Campbell Johnson, Negro head of reserve officer training at Howard University, had been made a special aide to draft director Lewis B. Hershey. Although Johnson previously had been asked to serve with Hershey and Davis was well qualified by experience for his promotion, the appointments had a strong political flavor when announced. In fact, FDR specifically directed that Davis's name be submitted for promotion, a military leader in a position to know told this writer.

---

[1] Patterson himself was reported by his associates at the time to be favorable to moves toward ending segregation, but was unable to make headway against the prevailing military opinion then current.

Roosevelt won the election, but the doors of war plants remained closed to Negroes and army segregation continued. By now, however, cracks were beginning to appear in the military's racial wall. Negroes had fought for and won a training school for Negro officers in World War I. But that war had demonstrated that separately trained Negro officers, admitted with lowered qualifications, were inadequate to command combat troops. Plans between wars specified that Negro officers, if any, must have identical training and standards with whites.

Available records, and recollections of officers at the time, indicated there apparently was little or no thought given to setting up separate Negro and white officer candidate schools at the start of World War II. Negroes from the start were assured an equal chance with whites to receive training, if qualified. Some Negro leaders sought a quota for Negro officers to assure them a fair share of officer opportunities. This was successfully resisted by army leaders who insisted officers could be selected only on "demonstrated qualities of leadership."

The unsegregated officer schools were the first significant step toward breaching the color line in the military establishment. Negro and white officer students, many of them college trained, studied and frequently lived together, among them Gordon Gray, a Carolinian who later became Secretary of the Army, and remembered his experiences.

A young white officer candidate from Atlanta, Georgia, according to Miss Byers' study, was horrified at having a Negro as one of the eight men in his hut at OCS, but three weeks later admitted liking the Negro better than any of the white candidates. In OCS at Camp Hood, a Negro was voted the most popular man in his class.

Other wartime breaks in the Army's segregation pattern were Dr. Paul R. Hawley's refusal to segregate Negroes in army hospitals in England, and an order in 1944 banning segregation in theaters, post exchanges, clubs and busses within army establishments. However, segregation in clubs on army bases continued to some degree, particularly in the South, under certain devices, such as setting aside one club for a particular unit — the units then being all-white or all-Negro.

On the dark side, there were numerous racial disturbances in the Army, some grave. The War Department's Troop Policies Committee under Assistant Secretary of War John J. McCloy, aided by Brigadier General Davis who served as a troubleshooter in the Army Inspector General's office, acted as a very busy fire brigade.

Negro leaders protested to no avail against the War Department policy of assigning large numbers of northern Negroes to southern posts, where most outbreaks occurred. General Marshall told this author later he "much regretted my decision acquiescing in the plan to train northern Negro units in the South, [a policy adopted] because of advantages to be gained in climate, economy, in construction, etc."

"It led to almost impossible situations in relation to local laws and conditions off the reservations," he said, "and added much to the bitterness of racial feelings."

In 1944, Army Service Forces headquarters in Washington authorized publication, despite sharp objections within the War Department, of Manual M-5, entitled "Leadership and the Negro Soldier." Efforts were made to suppress it after it was printed, and copies today are rare.

M-5 was the first successful attempt by Negro advisers in the War Department, working with officers favorable to equal treatment for Negroes, to air some of the favorable history of Negro soldiers and attack long-held dogmas about Negro inferiority. Its publication was bitterly fought by certain officers who believed Negroes to be inferior, and who saw the pamphlet as an attempt by "do-gooders" and politicians to improve the Negro at the expense of the Army. But the manual was issued. Sent to white officers of Negro troops, it did not openly oppose the War Department's segregation policy but stated: "The Army accepts no theories of racial inferiority or superiority for American troops, but considers its task is to utilize its men on their individual merits in the achievement of final victory."

The document turned the rays of latest scientific findings on the Army's long-befogged race problem, and helped lay the intellectual groundwork for the Army's eventual turnabout on segregation.

FIVE

"Are They Really Flying?"

Shortly before World War II, a Civil Aeronautics Administration inspector arrived at Tuskegee Institute, Alabama, to check upon Negro pilots being trained under the government's Civilian Pilot Training Program. The trainees were lined up, and the inspector singled out a seedy-looking youth in the back row wearing a straw hat.

A Pentagon official, relating the story in 1953, said the inspector took the Negro aloft and the young pilot appeared to follow instructions with hesitancy. Finally the inspector demonstrated a barrel roll, with the plane's nose pointing at the sun. The object was to test ability to keep on course, with the nose making as small a circle as possible around the sun.

The Negro appeared puzzled and asked the inspector to

repeat the demonstration. He did, and the youth asked for still another. Each of the three times the plane's nose described a small but definite circle about the sun. At length the young pilot said he guessed he could do it.

He promptly rolled the plane over, the nose never wavering off the sun. The amazed inspector asked him to do it again, whereupon he repeated the performance, then did it two or three times in the opposite direction. Finally he nosed the plane straight down, landing perfectly but with such abruptness that the inspector jumped out breathless.

The inspector walked up to the director of the training program. "You tricked me," he shouted.

He was right. The director had planted Charles Foxx, one of his star students, in the back row with a straw hat on his head. Foxx not only could fly; he became an instructor at the Army Air Corps training field for Negro pilots set up at Tuskegee in 1941.

Before World War II it was the consensus of military men that Negroes lacked technical ability to fly planes. Sharing that belief was Robert A. Lovett, Texas-born Assistant Secretary of War for Air and a pilot himself in World War I. Told during the early days of the Negro pilot program there was no scientific reason Negroes could not fly as well as whites, he reportedly replied, "No, I don't suppose so; there must be some emotional reason."

Under strong pressure from Negroes, who saw themselves being shut out of the new and glamorous Air Corps, and with the White House insistent, the Army in 1941 agreed to try the "experiment" of training Negro pilots.

Captain Noel Parrish, Kentucky-born Air Corps officer then adviser for a Negro Civilian Pilot Program unit in Chicago, was delegated to find a place in the vicinity to locate the Negro military field. More than one suburban community turned the proposition down despite the desire for an Air Corps school. Finally the Air Corps, strongly urged by the CAA, selected Tuskegee, where there was already a Negro Civilian Pilot Training Program.

Parrish, son of a minister of the Church of the Disciples of Christ and educated in the South, was described by those who knew him as a man of insatiable curiosity and interest in all kinds of people. After he was assigned to Tuskegee as head of the primary flying school, an assignment he was assured would be temporary, Parrish read Gunnar Myrdal's 1,483-page classic on American Negroes, *An American Dilemma*. He talked to every available anthropologist at the University of Chicago, consulted Negro and white newspaper editors, asked advice from northern and southern politicians. He had developed a firm conviction, based on his studies, that Negroes could fly just like other men if given sound training and favorable circumstances. He was determined to give each student a fair chance.

The new field at Tuskegee was ready to receive Negro trainees in July, 1941. Among the first to arrive was B. O. Davis, Jr., who had been serving as aide to his father, Brigadier General Davis, at Fort Riley, Kansas.

Young Davis, one of the few Negroes then to have graduated from West Point, had had a rough time at the Army's famed military academy. A fellow cadet, later a ranking army officer, described Davis's troubles. Upperclassmen, resenting a Negro in their midst, tried to force him out by giving him demerits for such things as imaginary flecks of dust on his shoes. But the West Point commander, Lieutenant Colonel Simon Bolivar Buckner, later to become a general and die a hero in World War II, told the seniors bluntly, "I'm not regulating your social life, but militarily, Davis is going to get the same here as everybody else." In December of Davis' first year, when he had been given more than enough demerits to oust him from the Academy, Buckner canceled half of them. The upperclassmen gave up their attempt, though Davis was ostracized throughout most of his four years.

But he showed no bitterness, proved himself a superior student and changed much of the hostility to admiration. Some of his own classmates quietly forced the more belligerent to stop hazing him. In his final year he asked for service in the Army Air Corps, only to be told by Buckner that the Air Corps admitted no Negroes and probably never would.

Discouraged, Davis went to the Army's Infantry School with the all-Negro 24th Infantry Regiment at Fort Benning, Georgia, and later served as his father's aide in Kansas. Offered a chance to join the first Negro Air Corps squadron at Tuskegee, he quickly accepted.

The Tuskegee "experiment" did not start off auspiciously. Some of the highest army and air corps officers expected, even hoped, it would fail. Colonel Frederick V. Kimble, first commander at Tuskegee and an old-line army officer, was not happy over his assignment and had little confidence in the Negroes. Following the traditional army pattern, he set up separate mess halls for Negroes and white officers sent to train them, and arranged separate toilet facilities.

Many Negro leaders condemned the Air Force for establishing a segregated base. Hastie, who had fought vigorously within the War Department against segregation policies, resigned in 1943 with an angry outburst against the Army and Air Corps, who had turned deaf ears to his protests against discrimination at Tuskegee.

But Parrish and the Negroes who went to Tuskegee kept

doggedly at their work. Davis, who was in the first group of five to graduate, was made commander of the proposed all-Negro 99th Pursuit Squadron, first Negro air unit in United States history. Repeatedly, he cited predictions of the squadron's failure as an incentive to spur the efforts of the often-discouraged trainees, exhorting them to prove the predictions false and bring honor to their race.

Some of the nearby residents refused at first to believe the Negroes were flying. One farmer asked Parrish, "Are those really Negroes up there or are you doing it for them?"

But the trainees surprised most of the officials who had set up the experiment. By October, 1942, enough pilots had graduated to complete, with Negro ground crews trained at Chanute Field, Illinois, the 99th Squadron. Months of frustration followed. The Negro press fought suggestions that the squadron be sent to Liberia, on grounds this would deprive it of combat. The military were afraid of "complications" in England. They waited until the North African invasion was a success; then in April, 1943, sent their problem child to French Morocco for a month's training under experienced combat fliers.

The squadron flew its first mission over an enemy air base at Fardjouna. It flew escort for dive bombers attacking the Mediterranean island of Pantelleria and escorted bombers over Italy. In mid-July, First Lieutenant Charles B. Hall bagged the first Axis plane officially credited to the squadron. Two of the 99th's planes were shot down that day.

During this period of relatively quiet support activity the squadron achieved little prominence, but in January, 1944, the 99th had its chance over the bitterly-contested Anzio beachhead. Negro pilots scored eight confirmed kills against 100 or more German Messerschmitts and Focke-Wulfs, the largest number then credited to any American squadron. *Time Maga-*

zine reported on February 14, 1944: "Any outfit would have been proud of the record. These victories stamped the final seal of combat excellence on one of the most controversial outfits in the Army, the all-Negro fighter squadron."

Meantime conditions had become progressively worse at Tuskegee. Negroes in training grew more bitter over continued discrimination. With Mrs. Roosevelt reportedly taking a hand, Kimble was replaced by Parrish, who had remained as head of the primary flying school. Conditions at Tuskegee gradually improved. Parrish, a natural diplomat, did not abolish the separate dining rooms outright, but said the Negroes would be served on the white side if they wished. Some of the white officers were bewildered; but Negro morale quickly rose. The Negro officers' club became one that all could join. Parrish joined it himself, and was frequently the only white man there.

The young Kentuckian not only got along with Negroes and white officers at the field, but helped explain the program to the fearful Tuskegee townspeople, nervously eyeing the armed Negroes. One night he received an urgent phone call from Davis, commander of the 99th Squadron. A Negro MP in town had been disarmed by reinforced white police after the MP had drawn a gun and forced them to release a Negro soldier. A group of Negro trainees at Tuskegee had got guns and headed for town in a truck.

Parrish leaped into his car and raced to Tuskegee Institute on the edge of town, where he met Davis. By luck, the Negroes had stopped there to find out what was happening in town. Parrish told them the Negro MP was in no danger, and promised to see he was not harmed. His known fairness and quiet persuasiveness sent the men back to their barracks.

Training continued, and sufficient Negro pilots and ground crews graduated to establish the 332nd all-Negro Fighter Group which was based at Selfridge Field, Michigan. Davis was re-called to take command and train it, and the group was sent overseas in January, 1944.

Brigadier General Ira S. Eaker, then Commander-in-Chief of the Mediterranean Allied Air Force, asked Davis if he wanted to continue air defense work or get into combat over Europe. Davis chose active combat with the 15th Air Force, then under Major General Nathan F. Twining, which was conducting long-range bombardment of Germany, Austria and Romania from bases in Italy.

The 332nd was given the Distinguished Unit Citation when, escorting a B-17 bombing raid on Berlin on March 24, 1945, it destroyed three German planes, probably destroyed another three and damaged three more without losing a single plane of its own. The official citation said that among the group's claims that day were "eight of the highly rated enemy jet-propelled aircraft. . . ."

Despite such performance records, there was continuing controversy in high military circles over the ability of the Negro airmen. But the Negroes, trained by conscientious white and Negro instructors and under Davis' highly respected leadership, had proved they *could* fly warplanes in combat.

Parrish said later it became clear to him toward the end of the war that an all-Negro organization would not fit into a highly complex Air Force. While attending the Air University at Maxwell Field, Alabama, Parrish wrote a thesis in May, 1947, that pointed directly at segregation itself as the chief remaining bar to the effective use of Negro airmen.

Meanwhile one of the 332nd's ace fliers, Captain Wendell 0. Pruitt, chalked up a record that was to bring him into dramatic contact with a man who would play a leading role in ending Air Force segregation. In addition to his German plane "kills,"

Pruitt led a fighter attack on an ammunition-laden German destroyer off the Istrian peninsula, and in one of the most spectacular single air strikes of the war, blew up and sank the ship — an almost unprecedented feat for a fighter plane. He had a meeting soon afterward with a St. Louis manufacturer — Stuart Symington — that was not forgotten when Symington became Air Force Secretary and helped change the complexion of the entire United States Air Force.

SIX

The Navy Charts a New Course

"By God," roared the navy captain, "I don't think a lieutenant like you should be allowed to question the judgment of captains and admirals."

Such a complaint was heard in the Navy's inner offices in Washington during World War II. The target was a young officer, entirely unprepossessing in appearance, who plotted and persuaded until the Navy adopted a racial policy so different from anything it had dreamed of that many of his superiors still blink in wonder.

Not that Lieutenant Chris Sargent did it all himself; far from it. But his influence radiated among a group of open-minded navy officials, from low-ranking but strategically placed officers up to Secretary James V. Forrestal; and the net result was an almost complete reversal of the Navy's segregation policies.

Son of an Episcopal minister, and former law clerk to Supreme Court Justice Benjamin Cardozo, Christopher Smith Sargent was commissioned in the Navy as a lieutenant (j.g.) in October, 1942. He was summoned from his job with Dean Acheson's law firm in Washington to the Navy's manpower division. He rose from a junior lieutenant to a full commander in two and a half years, and his influence on Navy racial policies is almost legendary.

Negroes had served in the Navy from the Revolution into the twentieth century with no distinction as to color, but limited to the ranks. Hardening of United States racial lines during the World War I period barred them from joining any but the Messman's Branch, where they soon were segregated, except for an increasingly small number of Negro gunners, oilers, cooks and other crew members left over from prewar days. Negroes were even barred from joining the Messman's Branch for a time between world wars, and none but Filipinos, Guamanians and other "brown-skinned" messmen were accepted — some of them still in the present-day Steward's Branch.

Frank Knox, Chicago publisher called in by FDR to run the Navy in World War II, stubbornly resisted efforts by Negro leaders and the President to give Negroes wider opportunities in the Navy. Knox, according to Navy records, said in explanation that the Navy had tried to man ships with Filipinos and Samoans after World War I but this had not worked and there was no reason to believe Negroes could sail ships either.

Outside pressure increased. Joe Louis boxed to raise funds for navy relief, and Wendell Willkie scored the Navy for accepting the Negro fighter's money while keeping Negroes in menial duties. Knox referred White House demands for action to special boards, which repeatedly came up with findings that the Navy's race policies were part of the national pattern and could not be changed without disrupting morale.

At length FDR, impatient, told Knox, "I think that with all the Navy activities, BuNav (Bureau of Navigation) might invent something that colored enlistees could do in addition to the rating of messmen." But Roosevelt agreed that "to go the whole way at one fell swoop would seriously impair the general average efficiency of the Navy."

Knox, who told associates that Negroes had rights and could not always be kept in second-class jobs, turned for help with this ticklish question to Adlai E. Stevenson, his Special Assistant, whom he had known in Chicago.

Stevenson, later to become the Democratic presidential nominee in 1952, sought to translate pressure from the White House and Negro groups into practical steps the Navy could undertake, according to officials close to him at the time. He considered it "ridiculous" that Negroes were not allowed to do anything but wait on tables, but told intimates it was quite a job to change some thinking in the Navy.

Stevenson discussed the problem with Sargent — whose influence was then beginning to be felt — and David K. Niles, White House specialist on minority problems. Finally the Navy agreed to use Negroes for additional duties, a step one official later described as "getting the first olive out of the bottle." The Navy said it might employ Negroes in labor and shore duties, and on non-seagoing craft, with "wide latitude" given to local commanders as to their numbers and use. To the latter part of the suggestion, FDR told Knox peremptorily in a memo, "This should be decided by you and me."

After conferring with Knox, FDR ordered a new program into effect. The Navy announced that beginning June 1, 1942,

Negroes could enlist for service other than messman duty. But they were segregated, and barred from seagoing vessels.

Under the new order, a historic step hailed by some Negro groups and denounced by others as still too restrictive, Negroes began training in segregated navy schools in Illinois and Virginia as gunners, clerks, signalmen, radio operators, etc. But many were given little opportunity to use their training, and were sidetracked into ammunition loading and construction battalions.

Meantime the Navy was forced by Paul V. McNutt's War Manpower Commission to begin accepting Negroes from Selective Service, which it had earlier refused to do. Starting in 1943, Negroes began pouring into the Navy in growing numbers, and officials were hard put to use them in the limited billets available.

Into this situation moved Sargent. His official job was assistant to the head of the Manpower Policies Section of the Planning and Control Division of the Bureau of Naval Personnel. The Negro problem landed squarely in his lap.

Bringing to his task an extraordinary adroitness of mind, persuasiveness and religious zeal, Sargent conceived the idea of a new unit to handle the Negro question. He picked Lieutenant Commander Charles M. Dillon, a Virginian then serving as Executive Officer of the Navy's Negro school at Hampton Institute, Virginia, to run what was named the "Special Programs Unit." Soon after, Lieutenant Commander D. Van Ness, stationed at the other navy Negro school at Great Lakes, Illinois, was brought to Washington. Van Ness and Dillon, informally sharing leadership of the Special Unit, put their heads together with Sargent.

Dillon said he himself was concerned chiefly with efficiency, and believed racial changes required careful experimentation before drastic steps were taken; Van Ness he labeled "something of a crusader"; Sargent, he added, was the spark plug of everything they did, believing "that here was a chance to prove we could all get along together in war when it couldn't be done in peace, and that it would reach into civilian society later."

Here, as Dillon and official records describe it, is how these three — with strong backing from James V. Forrestal when he became Secretary in 1944 — helped to steer the Navy into a new racial course.

On February 23, 1944, the Special Unit induced the Navy to put Negroes on two small seagoing craft, the new destroyer escort *U.S.S. Mason* and the submarine chaser *PC-1264*. They were manned entirely by Negroes with all-white officers save for one Negro.

But it soon appeared to the Special Unit that all-Negro ships were no solution to the Navy's problem. For one thing, there were not enough trained Negroes to handle the many jobs on ships. Six months after the all-Negro craft were launched, Dillon said his unit "decided we had to get them on ships without regard to race." He prepared a recommendation to mix Negroes with white crew members on twenty-five auxiliary ships of the fleet — tankers, oilers and similar vessels.

"There were objections from the enlisted men, who predicted all kinds of trouble, and some of the big guys jumped all over it," said Dillon. "Chris [Sargent] was there to ease their objections every time."

The Special Unit selected specific ships and jobs in which the Negroes were to be integrated, up to a maximum of 10 percent of the crews.

"It had to be ironclad so there would be no foul-up," Dillon explained. "We specified that none of the Negroes could be transferred without our approval, otherwise they'd soon all have been gone."

Dillon, to insure success, wanted to handpick the Negroes but was overruled with the argument that this would nullify the experiment. Instead a cross section of navy Negroes was called for, with no attention to their records except to assure competence in their respective ratings.

On May 20, 1944, James V. Forrestal, who had become Navy Secretary after Knox's death earlier that year, approved the proposal. The order, which went out to the twenty-five selected ships, called for "thorough indoctrination" of white personnel before the arrival of the Negroes.

Negro bluejackets, 15 percent of them third class petty officers from shore bases, 43 percent men from specialist schools and the remaining 42 percent from recruit training, were moved onto the auxiliaries.

According to official navy records, reports from many of the ships "showed that the colored general detail personnel were being successfully absorbed in the ships' companies." The skippers were polled and all but one reported favorably, according to an official observer.

From there it was only a step to putting Negroes on all fleet auxiliaries. The Special Unit noted in a memo February 7, 1945, that the Commander of Service Forces in the Pacific, Vice Admiral William L. Calhoun, had advised them of his belief that Negroes could be assigned to all auxiliary craft without difficulty, and that the Commander in Chief in the Pacific, Admiral Chester W. Nimitz, a Texan, had favorably endorsed this, providing it was done gradually. On April 13, 1945, a directive went out opening general ratings on all auxiliary vessels to Negroes.

Franklin D. Roosevelt, Jr., who commanded the *U.S.S. Ulvert M. Moore,* a destroyer escort, during the war, told this writer that a Negro cook was assigned to his ship, and two southern whites in the galley asked to be transferred because they would have had to serve under the Negro.

Roosevelt said he had a "fatherly talk" with the southern sailors, telling them the war was bigger than anyone's prejudices. "As it turned out," he said, "the old-timer was an excellent baker whose bread and cakes pleased the crew. He had a wealth of old-time navy sea stories with which he regaled his two white helpers and the rest of the ship's company, and before we reached the Panama Canal my racial problem had vanished and we had successfully integrated the galley personnel."

Jean S. Anderson, of Covington, Kentucky, a white machinist's mate aboard a Navy tanker, recalled the time the first Negro he ever saw outside the Messman's Branch came aboard his ship as a fireman. "When he came back to our division we told him there must be some mistake," related Anderson. "He said, 'The man told me to come back here.' We thought it pretty strange at first, but he was a nice sort of fellow, mixed right in with us, slept in the same compartment. I guess it takes all kinds to fight a war."

Lester Granger, Negro head of the National Urban League, a leading Negro organization, visited one of the auxiliary ships at Pearl Harbor. "The skipper, a southerner, showed me through with all kinds of pride," he related. "He said he'd been against it, didn't think it would work, but up to then there had been no incident to make him dissatisfied; he had to pinch himself to realize he had Negroes aboard."

Forrestal had been watching and approving. A former Wall Street broker with a reputation for lack of racial bias, he had long been a financial backer of the Urban League.

Somewhere around this time also, Stevenson, a confidant of Sargent, became close to Forrestal and exercised what one official of the time called a "constructive influence."

Rear Admiral Roscoe H. Hillenkoetter, who when a captain became Director of Planning and Control in the Personnel Bureau in 1944, recalled that shortly after he arrived Forrestal "called me over and said he wanted a study made of how to get away from segregation in the Navy."

Hillenkoetter told Forrestal he was a Missourian who had been brought up amid segregation and opposed doing away with it. He urged Forrestal to get someone else to make the study.

"Mr. Forrestal, however, ordered me to continue with it, and I went over the thing for about six months. At the end, I came up with what I now believe is the only answer possible; that is, there could be no discrimination or segregation in the Navy."

In 1945, following up on the study, Forrestal sent for Granger, who had been a fellow student at Dartmouth College, and secured his agreement to serve as a part-time navy consultant on racial problems. At his first meeting with Forrestal, Granger said the Secretary told him he was "very unhappy" with the present policy, under which large numbers of Negroes were still segregated in construction battalions and the Messmen's Branch. There had been riots and mutinies among segregated Negro units; on the other hand, Forrestal said, integration of Negroes with whites had been tried on smaller craft and had worked.

"He said he had taken it up with the President, who had given him carte blanche to go as far as he could," related Granger. Forrestal also said he had told Admiral Ernest J. King, then Chief of Naval Operations, "Admiral, I'd like to make a change in our racial policies. I can't do it without you fellows. The President wants it and I want it. How do you feel?"

King leaned back, Granger quoted Forrestal as saying, thought a bit and replied, "We say it's a democratic country; if so, we ought to have a democratic Navy. I don't know if we can do it, but if you want to try, I'll back you up every step of the way."

Forrestal told Granger, "All I can promise is that Denfeld (Admiral Louis E. Denfeld, then Chief of Naval Personnel), King and I will back you the whole way and between the three of us we can get the job done."

Forrestal arranged for Granger to tour navy bases throughout the United States and the Pacific, examine conditions and return with recommendations. Granger quoted Forrestal as saying, "You tell me. Go and see whatever you want. I ask one thing. If you see something is not right, give us a chance to set it straight before talking. If we are not honest about it, then tell the public."

Granger traveled 50,000 miles, visiting sixty-seven naval establishments in the United States and the Pacific. He talked to commanders, officers and men, and returned with a set of recommendations that added up to a policy of total nonsegregation in the Navy.

Forrestal was ready to move. On February 27, 1946, the following order went out to all naval stations and ships:

"Effective immediately, all restrictions governing the types of assignments for which Negro naval personnel are eligible are hereby lifted. Henceforth, they shall be eligible for all types of assignments in all ratings in all activities and all ships of the Naval Service. . . . In the utilization of housing, messing and other facilities, no special or unusual provisions will be made for the accommodation of Negroes."

Forrestal's deep insight into the far-reaching nature of racial problems was never more apparent than in a brief speech he made as Secretary of Defense in the spring of 1948 to a group of Negroes he had invited to the Pentagon to discuss military race policies. Forrestal said then:

"We're on an island in the world today which may either provide a beacon of hope or be engulfed by history, and the thing we're talking about is one of the milestones along that road."

Sargent, who is credited by an imposing number of high navy officials with being the guiding spirit behind the Navy's racial shift, died Christmas Eve, 1946, at the age of thirty-five, soon after seeing a new Navy launched for Negroes. He had just been made a full partner in Dean Acheson's law firm, and appeared headed for a brilliant career.

His father, pastor of St. Bartholomew's Episcopal Church in New York, read his congregation shortly after his son's death a sermon young Sargent had delivered at All Souls' Memorial Church in Washington in 1943.

"Few can be heroes, doing deeds of great import in a brief time," said Chris Sargent. "For us to serve must mean the accumulation of many little deeds and thoughts. Each Christian act we do, each high-aimed thought we go by, will add a bit to the Christian way."

SEVEN

The Negro Platoons

The winter of 1944 marked the beginning of the end for the Nazi war machine, which concentrated its might into a final, desperate effort to split Allied forces in France and Belgium. Slashing deep into Belgium, Field Marshal Gerd von Rundstedt's divisions threatened to drive to Antwerp, wipe out that vital Allied supply port and divide British-American armies in the north from French and American armies in the south.

Every available replacement was rushed to the front, but Allied commanders were woefully short of men. Bible-quoting Lieutenant General John C. H. Lee, then commander of U. S. Service Forces in the European Theater, proposed letting Negro service troops volunteer as riflemen. Having had thousands of them serving with him in England, Lee considered Negro troops "able-bodied, capable soldier material."

"They could shoot," he said later. "My chauffeur was a better shot than I. I had found them alert, willing, with good disciplinary and health records when under good leadership. And they knew how to handle weapons."

A man of deep religious convictions, Lee long had believed Negroes should have equal opportunities in the military; that they should be treated differently was to him a denial of teachings of the Bible. In England, with the vigorous support of Eisenhower, Supreme Allied Commander, Lee had clamped down on efforts of white officers to bar Negro GI's from associating with English civilians.

Officers put many English towns and pubs off limits to Negro soldiers. Stories were spread in England, as elsewhere in Europe, that Negroes were beasts with tails. Negroes, enraged by repeated discrimination, broke out in riots that were concealed under a cloak of strict military censorship. Lee took the matter up with Eisenhower and urged him to forbid discrimination. Eisenhower, according to Lee, replied that if Negroes were good enough to die in uniform, they were good enough to be entertained in uniform. Eisenhower issued an order, which Lee sent to every officer in England, emphasizing that the British had a different attitude toward race than many Americans, and that "considerable association of colored troops with British white population, both men and women, will take place on a basis mutually acceptable to the individuals concerned."

"Any attempt to curtail such association by official order or restriction is unjustified and must not be attempted," the order said.

Eisenhower sent for Brigadier General B. O. Davis, then attached to the Army Inspector General's Department in Washington, gave him copies of the order, and told him to visit all bases and see that it was carried out.

Lee visited bases together with the Negro officer. At one station the two inspecting officers called the commander's attention to reports he was giving his white and Negro soldiers passes to town on different days.

"I asked if he had read Ike's directive," said Davis. "He said, 'Oh, yes, we understand about those directives.' "

Lee asked, "You mean you're not taking the directives seriously?"

The commander replied knowingly, "We understand you have to issue those directives."

"Lee asked him how long it would take him to pack his trunk," Davis recalled. "He was promptly relieved, and so were many others who refused to obey."

According to General Davis, Lee — then commanding the Communications Zone in the European Theater — called Davis into his office when battle replacements were a burning problem and said he wanted to integrate Negroes with the white troops. Davis replied he had wanted that all along. Lee told him to prepare a directive.

Davis recalled that his proposal was to set up fifteen-man squads in which eleven men would be Negroes, with the squad leader, assistant squad leader and two experienced automatic riflemen whites. This was to provide battle-trained leadership and save the time it would take to train Negroes to use automatic weapons.

When the "Bulge" fighting was heaviest, according to Miss Byers' study, a letter went out to Negro service troops inviting volunteers to train as infantrymen and fight with white troops in the front lines. "It is planned to assign you without regard to color or race to units where assistance is most needed," it said.

Negroes rushed to volunteer. Sergeants gave up their stripes to qualify. In some rear-echelon units, Miss Byers reported that 80 percent of the men applied. Private First Class Leroy W. Kemp, a Negro ordnanceman, was quoted as saying, "We've been giving a lot of sweat. Now I think we'll mix some blood with it." So great was the press of volunteers that the number was finally limited to 2,500 lest the structure of Negro service units be disrupted. About 3,000 applications were turned down before the offer could be withdrawn.

On January 10, 1945, the volunteers began assembling at Noyons, France, for six weeks of training by battle-tried white officers and noncoms. The commander of the training center said, "These men will fight because they have been trained and treated just like the other soldiers here and they know they are going to be used in the same manner. . . ." When the first group went out, he said there were only two A.W.O.L. cases, and "we found out where the men were when we received a wire from a front line division commander informing us that they had reported to him to fight."

Meantime, however, the original plan to integrate the Negro volunteers in the same squads with combat-trained whites was changed. The War Department in Washington, getting wind of it, firmly turned thumbs down on any such radical steps. Overnight the original instructions were withdrawn from circulation and new orders were posted authorizing Negro platoons of some forty-eight men each to serve among white platoons, thus maintaining a degree of segregation.

General Eisenhower, as Supreme Allied Commander, approved the revised plan and the Negroes accepted it philosophically. The Negro platoons, commanded by combat experienced white officers, were rushed into action as elements of eleven divisions of the U.S. First and Seventh Armies. They quickly found themselves in the thick of fighting as, with the

Remagen bridgehead secured, the Allies completed their movement to the Rhine and began their push across Germany.

According to Lee, division commanders were "delighted" with the performance of the Negro platoons. He said Negro platoons of Major General Terry de la Mesa Allen's "Timberwolf" Division called themselves, "Black Timberwolves, de mos' fiercest of all Timberwolves." Commanders of the platoons themselves were generally favorable, though some units did not get into heavy fighting, a fact which led some officers later to disparage the entire "experiment."

But the most significant effect of the Negro platoons, where future policies were concerned, was their relations with white soldiers alongside whom they fought.

The Research Branch of the Army Information and Education Division of the European Theater sent fifty interviewers to question 250 white officers and enlisted men of seven of the divisions containing Negro platoons. The results were eye-opening. Eighty-six percent of the officers and 92 percent of the enlisted men felt that, with the same training and experience, Negro troops would be just as good as white troops. A large majority who had opposed serving in mixed units said they were "more favorable" to the idea after their experience.

A regiment commander commented, "I'm from the South — most of us here are — and I was pretty dubious as to how it would work out. But I'll have to admit we haven't had a bit of trouble." A platoon sergeant from South Carolina said when he first heard about the mixed service plan, he declared he'd "be damned if I'd wear the same shoulder patch they did; after that first day when we saw how they fought, I changed my mind; they're just like any of the other boys to us."

This study, added to growing evidence of the inefficiency of large, all-Negro units, pointed a clear way to more successful use of Negro soldiers. Davis and many others were anxious to have it published. Major General F. H. Osborn, Chief of the Information and Education Division, Army Service Forces, called the survey "of great interest" and urged its release to the public.

But General Brehon B. Somervell, Commander of Army Service Forces, questioned the advisability of publication. He said experience with a few volunteers was "hardly a conclusive test"; that Negro organizations might use the result to press for similar experiments with troops in training in the United States or operating in the Pacific; that publication might lose support for Universal Military Training, since many members of Congress, newspaper editors and other War Department friends "vigorously oppose mixing Negro and white troops under any conditions."

On August 25, General Marshall agreed that results of the study should not be released for publication "since conditions under which the platoons were organized were most unusual." He did, however, say that "the practicability of integrating Negro elements into white units should be followed up."[1]

While the platoons were the only formal experiments at racial integration of combat troops during the war, there were several "informal" incidents which left an indelible mark. The late General George S. Patton, who praised the Negro platoons assigned to the Third Army, put Negroes on his tanks when he raced through German lines in France.

Major General Anthony C. McAuliffe, famed for saying "Nuts!" to the German surrender demand at Bastogne, Belgium, found his ideas changing from the time when, as a

[1] Quoted in War Department documents in the files of the President's Committee on Equality of Treatment and Opportunity in the Armed Services (1949-50).

captain at the Army War College in 1939, he headed a sub-committee that recommended continued segregation. He re-called that after the "Bulge" was reduced he mounted white infantrymen on Negro-manned tanks that broke through the Siegfried Line. The combined teams "did an outstanding job, caught a lot of Germans," he said.

"They rolled ahead to a little German town where they stopped for three or four days. I watched them fraternizing, cooking and eating out of the same pans. When I saw that I knew it would work."

McAuliffe did not know then that he would be given the job five years later of bossing the Army's program of eliminating all segregation from its ranks for good.

EIGHT

Air Force: New Pilot, New Policy

Despite holes in the military color dike, Negro leaders at the close of World War II had little hope of an early change in the basic pattern of military segregation. Lieutenant General John C. H. Lee said it was a "bitter regret" to him that the Negro platoons were not allowed to come home with the white divisions in which they served.

Negro soldiers returning to their homes in the South met some of the same treatment that followed World War I. Isaac Woodward, Negro veteran of Pacific jungle fighting, was en route to his home in North Carolina when the driver of his bus asked the police chief in a South Carolina town to arrest him for drunken disorderliness.

In vain Woodward protested he did not drink. The chief

beat him with a blackjack and struck his eyes with a night stick, blinding him for life. The case caused national stir.

Negro leaders carried the details to the White House in a drive to get support for legislation against mob violence.

Walter White, who headed the Negro delegation, said in his autobiography that President Truman listened grimly as White told of lynchings in Georgia and Louisiana, of the fresh flood of hate literature, and the blinding of Isaac Woodward.

He quoted the President as saying, "My God! I had no idea it was as terrible as that. We've got to do something."

David K. Niles, Mr. Truman's chief adviser on minorities, suggested a committee to investigate civil liberties violations and to propose corrections. The Negro delegation was skeptical, recalling similar proposals by FDR that came to nothing. But this time the outcome was President Truman's noted Commission on Civil Rights, headed by Charles E. Wilson of General Electric Company, whose findings formed the basis for Mr. Truman's vigorous civil rights program — a program which led to a Southern Democratic split in 1948 that almost cost the President his re-election. It was this commission that publicized the long-suppressed survey of the Negro platoons in World War II.

The Navy, meanwhile, was moving quietly ahead with its new racial policy, but the Army emerged from the war more puzzled than ever about Negro troops. Some in its councils felt the need for a drastic change, but others in high places resisted all suggestions of ending segregation.

In the late fall of 1945, the War Department set up a special three-man board of officers to restudy the problem of Negro troops. Headed by Lieutenant General Alvan C. Gillem, a southerner, it found ample evidence that small composite infantry companies, such as Negro platoons in white companies, were "eminently successful when ably led."

It recommended continuation of such groupings, and use of qualified Negroes in "overhead" duties at military posts — clerical, supervisory and maintenance — without regard to race. While the board said the "ultimate objective" in another war should be use of all army manpower "without regard to antecedents or race," it avoided specific proposals for ending segregation.

Although the Army opened some new opportunities to Negroes as a result of the Gillem Board's recommendations, which were approved by General Dwight D. Eisenhower, then Army Chief of Staff, there was continued opposition within the Army to putting even these limited proposals into effect.

But the Air Force, newly launched as an independent service in 1947, was incubating its own ideas. As part of the Army, the Air Corps had followed the Army's segregation policy for years. But after September 18, 1947, when Stuart Symington became the first Air Secretary with Lieutenant General Idwal S. Edwards his personnel chief, a drastic new pattern swiftly took form.

Symington, born in Amherst, Massachusetts, was the son of an Amherst College professor and grandson of a Confederate Army soldier. He grew up in a home free from racial bias, where help for Negroes was stressed.

Graduating from Yale University, Symington entered the business world and his unusual executive ability brought him rapid advances. In 1938 he took over the declining Emerson Electric Manufacturing Company in St. Louis and rebuilt it into a multimillion-dollar business. In the process he was credited with the first substantial use of Negroes in skilled industrial work in St. Louis.

Symington was a member of St. Louis Mayor Aloys P. Kaufman's committee on race relations. On December 12, 1944, the city celebrated "Captain Wendell O. Pruitt Day" in honor of the first Negro fighter pilot from St. Louis to return from overseas.

The mayor brought Pruitt, who had achieved an enviable combat record including the sinking of a German destroyer, to see Symington, who said, "Pruitt, I'm proud to be a member of the same country as you. What can I do for you?"

"Give my people a chance," was Pruitt's reply.

"I might have told him we already had," said Symington later, "but I didn't think it was fitting." Pruitt that day appeared nervous, and Symington felt he should have given up flying. A few weeks later the Negro airman was killed in a plane crash at Tuskegee, but his plea was not forgotten.

Shortly after Symington became Air Secretary, James C. Evans, Negro Civilian Assistant to the Secretary of Defense, came to ask what he planned to do about Negroes in the Air Force. Evans, son of a Baptist minister, had spent six years in the office of Truman Gibson, War Department racial adviser.

Symington told Evans he believed Negroes in the Air Force should have whatever they could get on merit. "If there's anything wrong, see Gene," he said, pointing to his Assistant Secretary, Eugene Zuckert. "If you don't get what you want, my door is always open."

Symington recalled that he used to meet Evans in the hall, and say, "Why don't you come to see me?" He said Evans would reply, "I don't have anything to see you about — you're doing all right."

Symington directed Zuckert to see what could be done to equalize opportunities for Negroes. The first step was opening the Aviation Cadet training program, the Air Force's officer training setup, to qualified Negroes on an unsegregated basis.

Evans visited Randolph Field, Texas, reporting on his return that he was gratified to find nine Negroes in unsegregated aviation cadet training. Relaying this to Symington, Zuckert got back a terse memo: "Gene: Why not more?"

Even before Symington became Air Secretary, there were signs within the Army Air Force of a shift in thinking on racial policy. This was fortified on March 1, 1948, by a memo from General Edwards, personnel chief, declaring it to be the "feeling of this office that it should be the ultimate Air Force objective to eliminate racial discrimination and segregation among its personnel by the unrestricted assignment of Negro personnel in free competition with white personnel to any duty in the Air Force for which they qualify." It proposed a "gradual" shift.

Edwards, born in Freedom, New York, and also the son of a Baptist minister, long had believed segregation was a waste of manpower. A long-time army officer, he served on the World War II Army Troop Policies Committee, headed by Assistant Secretary of War John J. McCloy, that took many steps to end discrimination against Negroes.

Testifying in April, 1948, at a meeting of Negro leaders called to the Pentagon by Secretary of Defense Forrestal to discuss military racial policies, Edwards said he did not agree with many Air Force officers that mixing in Negroes would demoralize white units.

Asked if he would rather deal with segregated units or manpower as such in another way, Edwards replied, "Frankly, I would prefer the utilization of manpower." But in a note to Symington after the conference, he said he had found solid opposition among Air Force officers to integrating Negroes and whites in the same units.

Nevertheless, under Symington's prodding, Zuckert's deputy, Clarence Osthagen, and Lieutenant Colonel Jack Marr, an ex-combat pilot, were put to work seeking a way out of Air Force segregation. Marr and Osthagen read Colonel Noel Parrish's challenging thesis on Negroes, pointing at segregation itself as the major obstacle to full use of Negroes and ridiculing many racial misconceptions that marked traditional military thinking. Preliminary work had been begun on a new Air Force policy, with stubborn resistance from many officers, when the whole atmosphere was electrified by an Executive Order from President Truman. Dated July 26, 1948, it provided that henceforth there should be "equality of treatment and opportunity for all persons in the armed services without regard to race, color, religion or national origin."

Symington, who with Forrestal had participated in spade work on the order, related later that he went to the White House after its issuance and asked the President, "Will you back me up?"

"With no reservation," said Harry Truman.

Symington summoned his generals.

"We're going to end segregation," he said. "Those are my orders from the Commander-in-Chief. You've got to stop the double talk and act."

Edwards promised his full support.

There were alarmed reactions from some Air Force officers, who predicted serious disturbances. Symington was adamant. General Hoyt S. Vandenberg, Air Force Chief of Staff, and many other Air Force leaders were willing to give the new policy a fair test. Edwards put Marr to work preparing the actual program for wiping out the Air Force color line.

Osthagen worked with Marr on the program. Zuckert kept pushing them ahead, holding many conferences with Marr to work out some of the "tough" spots.

Marr's resultant study, a painstaking work that took months to complete, pointed out that many potential skills were being lost in a segregated Air Force. He gave as an example a Negro rated both as an aerial gunnery instructor and a navigator-bombardier. Neither of these skills was needed at the all-Negro air base at Lockbourne, Ohio, where the Tuskegee experiment had moved in 1946 and where the Negro fighter wing was stationed; yet the Air Force elsewhere was "woefully short" of such men.

Marr noted that where qualified Negroes had been permitted to compete on the basis of individual ability, they had achieved a "certain amount" of acceptance. He referred specifically to integration in the Navy, where he noted that, outside the Steward's Branch, "no distinction is made between Negro and white sailors" and there were few reported difficulties.

Declaring that Air Force personnel planning must be done on the basis of judgment and facts, not tradition or emotion, Marr said that keeping the old racial policy would mean "continuing and increasing monetary waste and loss of tactical efficiency as well as providing various pressure groups and agitators with continual and justifiable reasons for criticism."

He concluded by saying, "Fears of social and morale difficulties are largely imaginary." Few Air Force leaders, including Edwards, who approved the plan, believed it would be quite that easy, but Marr's words proved prophetic.

One hurdle remained. Army Secretary Kenneth C. Royall, a North Carolinian who saw the long-range value of ending segregation but was not ready to go the whole way, complained in a letter to Secretary of Defense Forrestal that the Air Force was trying to show up the Army. He said the Air Force didn't really intend to end segregation. General Vandenberg replied in a memo to Forrestal that the Air Force did indeed "mean it."

Symington and his staff waited from December, 1948, until April, 1949, when Louis Johnson, who had succeeded the ailing

Forrestal, overrode Royall's protests and approved the new plan.

On May 11, the Air Force announced its new policy. Segregation was to be eliminated by swift, planned stages. The Negro base at Lockbourne, Ohio, was to be broken up, and its men sent to air bases throughout the world, routed to technical schools for further special training, or dismissed if they had nothing to offer an integrated Air Force. The policy did not specify that all-Negro units must be abolished completely, but it worked out that way.

By the end of 1949, Lockbourne's Negroes had gone and most air bases had become integrated. By the end of 1952, the Air Force could boast that it was the only branch of the armed services with no all-Negro components left.

General Vandenberg said later that the Air Force integration program — as far as he was concerned — was *not* undertaken solely in the interest of military efficiency; "it was a bold attempt to tackle a broad-gauged national problem" — racial segregation itself.

NINE

Truman: Politics and Principle

Look back now to May, 1939. Two Negro WPA workers, who learned to fly in their spare time, took off that month from Chicago in an open, two-seater biplane for Washington to lobby for inclusion of Negroes in the government's Civilian Pilot Training Program.

A broken crankshaft forced the fliers, Chauncey E. Spencer and Dale L. White, to land in an Ohio farmer's back yard. They waited two days for friends to raise fifty-four dollars for a new crankshaft, then resumed their flight. Lacking navigation instruments or radio, they landed in the dark at the Pittsburgh, Pennsylvania, county airport behind an incoming commercial plane. Temporarily grounded, they were cleared the next morning and finished their trip to Washington.

Edgar Brown, bearded Negro lobbyist, took them to Capitol

Hill and stopped a senator walking down a corridor. Introducing the fliers, Brown told their story dramatically. That senator was Harry S. Truman.

The Senator from Missouri replied that if they had guts enough to do all that, he had guts enough to back them. True to his word, Truman helped put through legislation to assure training for Negroes as well as whites under the Civilian Pilot Training Program. Some of the Negroes thus taught to fly helped launch the all-Negro 99th Pursuit Squadron at Tuskegee, Alabama, two years later.

Opening his Senate re-election campaign at Sedalia, Missouri, June 15, 1940, Truman said: "In giving Negroes the rights that are theirs, we are only acting in accord with our ideals of a true democracy."

In the White House some seven years later, President Truman received the report of his Civil Rights Commission calling for drastic action to secure equal rights for Negroes, including both legislative and executive action to banish segregation from the armed forces.

Clark Clifford, then special counsel to the President, said later that Truman, when he received the Commission's report, wanted to send a message to Congress at once.

"He talked to me about the tremendous experiment in government our forefathers believed in, how they were afraid of setting up a nobility," said Clifford. "He was very conscious of their thinking — that in a democracy of this kind, each man was a political entity equal to every other man. If the American experiment was to work, he felt this must not be idle words in political speeches, but action."

He said the President also felt strongly that this country's failure to assure equal rights to Negroes was one of its weakest points in the struggle with Communism.

Clifford was assigned to "rough out" the President's civil rights message. What emerged was a strong program, but less drastic than advocated by the Civil Rights Commission.

"The President felt you had to proceed by gradual stages; it would be better assimilated that way, with much better chance of ultimate success," recalled Clifford.

Yet even that gradual program brought a Southern Democratic cyclone about the President's head when his civil rights message was read to Congress. Among other things, it called for federal legislation to curb lynching, ban poll taxes and assure fair employment rights to all. It did not request legislation to bar segregation in the armed forces; this was left for presidential action.

Not only the southerners turned away from Truman in the spring of 1948. Many party stalwarts, including liberals and "machine" Democrats, were beginning to look for a new leader. A few stalwarts stuck by, including Oscar R. Ewing, a New Yorker who was Truman's Federal Security Administrator.

Ewing said later it had become obvious to him after the 1946 election, in which the Republicans won control of Congress, that Truman had not caught on with the voters. He said, "l felt we had to build him up as the champion of various groups." He and others close to the President discussed this problem repeatedly as Truman's influence waned in 1948.

At the Democratic convention in Philadelphia in July, Truman smothered attempts to dump him and won his party's nomination. Hubert H. Humphrey of Minneapolis helped force through one of the most drastic civil rights planks in Democratic history. It called, among other things, for the right of "equal treatment in the service and defense of our nation."

Back in Washington after the convention, Ewing told the President he must immediately do everything within his power as Chief Executive to carry out the civil rights provisions of the Democratic platform. Otherwise, he said the Democrats would lose the Negro vote. "There was never a question where Truman stood," Ewing added later. "Any question he had was how far he could go."

Truman himself, discussing the 1948 situation with this author after he had left the White House, said he had served next to the all-Negro 92nd Division in World War I and had seen what happened. The Negro 93rd Division, whose four regiments served under the French, was "100 percent all right" but elements of the 92nd did not measure up in combat, he recalled.

Curious as to the reason, he said he made his own inquiries after the war, discussing the question with reserve officers who had served with both divisions. He was particularly concerned over the contrasting performance of two divisions, one segregated under American leadership and the other unsegregated as regards officers under French practices. He concluded that nonsegregation was the answer because that was the only way in which ability and training were the sole basis for selecting leaders.

With this behind him and the election coming on, Truman decided to issue two executive orders. Philleo Nash, White House specialist on minorities, was summoned by plane from his Wisconsin cranberry farm, and he, Clifford, Ewing and others worked furiously drafting the orders. Nash said he had previously contemplated a committee within the military establishment to push steps toward nonsegregation, similar to the War Department's Troop Policies Committee in World War II. He now urged immediate creation of such a committee, with presidential appointees as members to give it stature and authority. "Let the committee find out in each branch where segregation hurts efficiency," he advised; "don't spell it out in advance."

Symington, Forrestal and others were consulted. Forrestal, according to Marx Leva, then his special assistant, urged that the order call for progress "as rapidly as feasible," rather than laying down any flat edict, believing this would give the services a chance to work out methods of compliance rather than rousing their antagonism. Truman agreed to this approach.

Before the order was issued, Ewing took it to Forrestal for military clearances. Ewing said Forrestal was "sure" there would be no objection from Symington or Secretary of the Navy John L. Sullivan, but asked Ewing himself to take it up with Secretary of the Army Royall.

Ewing took the order to Royall, whom he quoted: "Will you tell the President that I not only have no objections, but wholeheartedly approve, and we'll go along with it?"

Royall, however, may have understood the order as less of a signal for swift action toward complete integration than did Stuart Symington.

On Monday, July 26, the President issued two executive orders, one setting up new machinery to halt discrimination in federal employment, the other dealing with the armed services. The second, bearing the undistinctive title "Executive Order 9981," began: "It is essential that there be maintained in the armed services of the United States the highest standards of democracy, with equality of treatment and opportunity for all those who serve in our country's defense."

Calling on the President's dual authority as Chief Executive and Commander in Chief of the armed forces, it laid down two major provisions:

1. "It is hereby declared to be the policy of the President that there shall be equality of treatment and opportunity for all per-

sons in the armed services without regard to race, color, religion or national origin. This policy shall be put into effect as rapidly as possible, having due regard to the time required to effectuate any necessary changes without impairing efficiency or morale." (There was to be sharp controversy later as to how far this required the military to go.)

2. It created the "President's Committee on Equality of Treatment and Opportunity in the Armed Services," and directed it to check into practices of each service "in order to determine in what respect such rules, procedures and practices may be altered or improved with a view to carrying out the policy of this order."

At his first news conference after the order was issued, the President emphasized that he expected all racial segregation to be abolished eventually from the armed services.

The committee was not appointed until October and did not meet until January. Its fate, had not Truman won the election, is open to conjecture. The part the racial orders played in the election is hard to weigh. Ewing, who backed them as a political imperative, said, "We suddenly felt things clicking around October, when people began saying, the little guy is in there fighting for us."

Nash , too, felt the President's civil rights stand had a part in winning the election, showing the voters he had "guts" and could control his own party.

Some have declared that Truman's civil rights program, as well as his consistent votes for racial rights measures in the Senate, were based largely on political motives. His intimates say his record demonstrates the falseness of this view. Nash said that the role of the equal rights directives in the 1948 election "shows the importance of politics in making progress toward American ideals."

"To meet the challenge of the Democratic platform, after a convention fight, required the Chief Executive to take action," he said. "Thus political necessity dictated the timing for steps on which much patient preparation had been made, and provided the opportunity to accomplish the results the President wanted."

TEN

The Fahy Committee

The success of any program is often determined by the men picked to carry it out. President Truman and his White House staff figured long and carefully on the make-up of the new Committee on Equality of Treatment and Opportunity in the Armed Services. It was David Niles who first suggested as chairman Charles Fahy, Georgia-born Catholic and former U.S. Solicitor General, who had performed many delicate missions, including a role in securing United States use of British Caribbean bases for the loan of American destroyers during World War II.

Fahy had a fatherly smile and a gentle, almost inaudible way of talking, but packed what Nash called "the punch of a mule." Niles described him as "totally reconstructed on the subject of race."

Other members of the committee were Dwight R. G. Palmer, president of the General Cable Corporation in New York, a board member of the Urban League and an active campaigner for racial equality in employment; Alphonsus Donahue, a prominent Catholic layman, who died before the committee finished its work; Lester Granger, chosen partly for his closeness to Forrestal as one of two Negroes on the committee; William E. Stevenson, president of Oberlin College, which had a long tradition of non-discrimination; John H. Sengstacke, Negro publisher of the *Chicago Defender;* and Charles Luckman of Lever Brothers, who did not take part in the committee's work. The story of the committee's often stormy career was told this writer by leading participants.

Fahy went to see President Truman at the start and said he wanted to try to reach agreement with the services rather than lay down the law to them; he said it would take time. The President approved his plan of action.

The committee, plunging into its work, had no serious controversies with the Navy or Air Force. It found that the Navy, in a five-year period, had "moved from a policy of exclusion of Negroes from general service to one of complete integration in general service." However, it expressed concern at the small numbers of Negroes and Negro officers in the Navy, and at the fact that noncommissioned officers in the Steward's Branch received "the pay and the perquisites, but not the grades" of petty officers in the rest of the Navy. It felt that the small percentage of Negroes in general service ratings could be traced in part to "a long memory of the Navy's earlier restrictive policy and to a general unawareness among Negroes that this policy had been discarded."

It made four recommendations: that the Navy, in its recruiting literature and press releases, stress its policy of using Negroes on the same basis as whites in general service; that a number of Negro reserve officers be called to active duty to speed recruiting of Negroes; that the Navy take positive steps to inform Negro high school and college students of the Naval Reserve Officers Training Corps program; and that chief stewards be given the grade of chief petty officer.

The Navy accepted all the recommendations on June 7, 1949; but it made slow headway in increasing the number of Negro bluejackets and officers.

The Air Force, using the President's Executive Order to overcome remaining opposition, was then completing work on its new non-segregation policy. After one session with Air Force officials, the committee agreed to avoid making any recommendations until the Air Force was ready with its own plan. This, with some changes proposed by the committee, such as elimination of a quota for Negroes, later proved completely acceptable.

But with the Army it was a different story. Army Secretary Kenneth C. Royall, in a statement to the committee in March, 1949, said the Army was "not an instrument for social evolution" and added that experience in two wars showed Negro troops to be less qualified than whites for service in combat. He repeated his proposal for a "voluntary experiment" in non-segregation, which was rejected the previous year by the Navy and Air Force as little more than a gesture. He stressed the fact that the Army had vastly more Negro officers than either the Navy or Air Force, and said he intended further to increase the number in the Army.

Royall resigned in early 1949 and was replaced as Army Secretary by Gordon Gray, a North Carolina lawyer, newspaperman and legislator who had been serving as an Assistant Army Secretary. Gray, described by intimates as a tough but fair-minded southerner, indicated to the committee at first that he did not intend to be pushed into any "adventures." Army experts, appearing before the committee, maintained that the Army was already giving Negroes the "equal treatment" prescribed by the President's order, even under a segregated system.

E. W. Kenworthy, Executive Secretary of the Fahy Committee, recalled later that the committee sparred almost continuously with army officers who tried to mislead it about the Army's handling of Negroes. He said one army representative telephoned him more than once to say, "Well, you saw through that gimmick, but we'll think up another one that will stop you."

At one point Worthington Thompson, special assistant to Defense Secretary Louis Johnson, had Kenworthy redpencil a lengthy list of "misinformation" contained in official army statements to the committee. This was relayed to Gray, and committee members said Gray later admitted to them apologetically that his own officers had misled him.

Efforts by certain army officers to sabotage steps toward non-segregation reached a climax in October, 1949, after Gray had agreed to abolish Negro quotas for army schools and to open military occupational specialties to qualified men "without regard to race or color."

The new order went out on October 1, 1949. Some weeks later Kenworthy found in his desk drawer a copy of a second order, placed there by an unknown informant. The second order, dated October 27, said the previous order was "not intended . . . (to) be interpreted to authorize *assignments* to troop vacancies without regard to race or color." Flatly contradicting Gray's order, it said Negroes would be assigned only to "authorized Negro vacancies."[1]

[1] Italics mine. Author.

That was one of the few details of the behind-the-scenes struggle that was "leaked" to the press. The next day the *Washington Post* published a sharp editorial saying Gray was getting the runaround from his own officers.

"Gray was furious," recalled Kenworthy. "The colonel who wrote that second order was on his way that very day." An official army press release, dated November 3, quoted Gray as saying the second order violated the Army's announced policy and "as soon as it came to his attention he ordered it rescinded."

The turning point of the committee's wrestling match with the Army was the appearance of Roy Davenport, a scholarly Negro army personnel technician. Davenport was one of the few men in the Army, Negro or white, who knew the facts and figures on treatment of Negroes and could explain precisely why existing conditions amounted to serious discrimination. Committee members had met him, but remained unaware of the key role he could play in their deliberations. James C. Evans, Defense Department racial adviser, deliberately sought to push Davenport before the committee.

Finally, flanked by two other army personnel experts and loaded with charts and tables, Davenport appeared formally at a committee hearing. Fahy had considerable difficulty understanding the technical explanations. Other committee members grew restive, proposed adjournment. Fahy, insisting that Davenport continue, at last began to see daylight. Davenport and his colleagues were demonstrating precisely how segregation slammed the door on equal opportunity for Negro soldiers despite official statements to the contrary.

Here was the reason: Previous army spokesmen had insisted that any soldier, regardless of race, was free to attend any army school to learn skills such as electronics, weather observations, radar, etc. But — to be sent to a school, there must first be job openings that would use the acquired skill. All-Negro units, small in size and limited in nature, provided few opportunities to use most army-taught skills. Thus Negroes, who for the most part would have to return to Negro outfits, had little or no chance to go to specialist schools.

The hearing over, Fahy went into conference with Gray and General J. Lawton Collins, Army Chief of Staff. Quietly but insistently he laid before them the picture he had discovered. The Secretary said if this condition were ended, it would force the breakup of segregated units. Fahy agreed. But he said it would mean using Negroes on the basis of proved ability and training, and predicted white soldiers would readily accept Negroes with the same preparation as themselves.

Leveling a finger at Gray and Collins, Fahy said if a Negro with the same ability as a white man went to school and learned to be a skilled radar operator, he should be given a radar operator's job regardless of his race. He cited the Navy's experience, where men were living together in close quarters aboard ship, and the Air Force's then-active integration movement.

Meanwhile Davenport, deeply upset by the misinformation army officials had given the committee, took up the problem with Evans, the Defense Department racial adviser, who discussed it with Gray's Special Assistant, James F. King, who arranged a meeting between Davenport and Gray in December, 1949.

In an extraordinary hour and twenty minute session, Davenport said he repeated frankly to Gray his belief that the Army was misleading the Fahy Committee. Gray asked for an example. Davenport offered a statement given to the committee over Gray's signature. It reported, as progress made under the President's order, the establishment of a single promotion system in the Army's career guidance program, without regard to race. This system, said Davenport, actually had been established considerably before the President's order.

Gray, alerted to the possibility of misleading language, outlined to Davenport his program for complying with the President's directive, and asked him to put it in language of a personnel technician to assure its accomplishment.

As recalled by Davenport, the Secretary said he wanted to assure every individual a post that would make maximum use of his ability, approaching that goal in a gradual manner with careful trial to be sure it would work. He wanted to start with the higher skills and work down until only basic training remained to be integrated, and added the time would come when segregation could be ended in basic training.

Davenport and others sweated over the precise language that would carry out Gray's proposals. When it was ready, Davenport urged the Fahy Committee to accept it as a real advance toward the goal of non-segregation. The committee promptly agreed.

The heart of the new policy statement, formally issued by the Army on January 16, 1950, was that Negroes with special skills would be "assigned to any . . . unit without regard for race or color." Davenport explained that "assigned" was the critical word; Negroes had theoretically been eligible for special training, but could not be assigned to white units where they might use their skills.

There was sharp controversy over the effectiveness of the President's order and the committee's work, particularly in regard to the Army. Some of the highest ranking army officials maintained that the President's order did not require an end to segregation, and that the Fahy Committee did little or nothing to move the Army on the road to non-segregation. Fahy and others were equally convinced that Truman's order, backed by the committee actions, played an important role in getting the Army to shake loose from its firm insistence on segregation.

There was almost universal agreement that, in any case, the Army would not have moved with the speed it did toward non-segregation had not the Korean War broken out in June, 1950. Military leaders, including General Omar N. Bradley, Chairman of the Joint Chiefs of Staff until August, 1953, said the war hastened army integration by at least ten years.

Truman, in the early summer of 1953, gave this author his own judgment of the overall effect of the military integration program.

He said it meant the nation was approaching a point where race superiority would no longer exist, where people would recognize that the human animal was the same, with the same feelings and emotions' no matter what his skin color.

"It's the greatest thing that ever happened to America," Harry Truman declared.

ELEVEN

No Problem, Gentlemen

In late June, 1949, a mother in Bristol, Tennessee, received an anguished letter from her son in the Air Force: "Mom, this is something I want you or Dad to do quick. They are mixing the niggers in the same barracks with us. If everyone's parents write their congressmen to ask for something to be done about it, it will. Mom, please don't let me down. Quick! "

The mother promptly wrote her congressman to say her son's letter "raised my southern blood to the boiling point. . . . The nation has enough international headaches without starting a revolution here at home. . . ."

She was not alone in her fears when the Air Force, in May, 1949, began putting into effect its new integration policy, just approved by Defense Secretary Louis Johnson. Many Air Force officers, particularly southerners, were certain the radical departure from past practices would start a chain reaction of riot, disruption and desertion. Many Negroes themselves were fearful of the new program, doubtful they would have a fair chance in a white Air Force.

But the Air Force moved aggressively ahead. A board of officers, on which Colonel B. O. Davis, Jr., served, began screening Negro airmen at Lockbourne, Ohio, on May 16. Those considered suitable for immediate assignment to existing units were shipped to air bases throughout the world. Those with potential skills were sent to Air Force schools to learn radar, photography, weather observation. Those not measuring up to standard were honorably discharged. Negro service-type units at other bases were similarly screened and broken up.

Air Force commanders throughout the world were carefully prepared for the new step. Lieutenant General Idwal Edwards, Air Force personnel chief, told all commanders they were expected to use sense in putting the program into effect, but warned that failure to act promptly would be considered a "command failure." An additional directive called for "prompt disciplinary action" against any effort to disobey the integration order.

Preparations by commanders to handle the new problem varied. Lieutenant General Lawrence Kuter, then head of the Military Air Transport Service, laid down perhaps the sternest line in a letter to all MATS commanders that stated: "Commanders who cannot cope with the integration of Negroes into formerly all-white units or activities will have no place in the Air Force structure." Most commanders held lengthy conferences with their senior officers, carefully briefed their white airmen and noncommissioned officers, and mapped careful procedures to deal with any trouble. Apprehension reached the point where, at Keesler Air Force Base, Biloxi, Mississippi, plans were in readiness to spirit the Negroes away from the area instantly in event of hostilities by whites from the base or adjacent town.

Other leaders took the attitude that to prepare for trouble would invite it. Brigadier General Carl B. McDaniel, commander at Mather Air Force Base in California, was asked at a staff meeting shortly before Negroes were integrated whether serious consideration should not be given to the coming problem.

"Gentlemen," said the commander, refusing to discuss the issue, "there is no problem." And there was none at Mather, according to a staff officer there at the time.

General Edwards said later he felt that a strong, positive policy, firmly backed from Washington, would put the new program across.

"A boy born in Mississippi is not going to support something contrary to his upbringing if he isn't given strong command direction," he explained. But under a firm directive, if commanders received local complaints, they could reply they had to obey orders.

Anxious to keep tight rein over the program, Edwards wrote to all Air Force commanders on July 21 asking them for full reports on the progress of integration. The replies, unsensational in themselves, constitute an extraordinary documentation of a remarkable social change.

On August 4 came the first significant response. The Air Proving Ground Headquarters at Eglin Air Force Base in Florida reported it had encountered only "minor problems." Commanders and staff, it said, had given the program complete cooperation; no difficulties had been encountered or expected and the Negroes were being kept carefully "spread."

Then followed in swift succession letters which showed that the experiment was succeeding beyond the most optimistic hopes. A typical report, from Major General Robert W. Harper, head of the Air Training Command, said that Lackland Air Force Base, giant basic training center at San Antonio, Texas, had been training airmen without racial distinction for more than two months with "no racial disturbance in any phase . . . on or off duty."

Corroborating reports followed from overseas. General George E. Stratemeyer wrote on September 16 that integration was progressing smoothly in his Far Eastern Air Force. Scattered indignation among white airmen, he said, had changed to passive acceptance or "lively interest" when it became clear the Air Force really was going through with its announced plan, and reaction was even more favorable when Negro airmen arrived.

On September 17 Lieutenant General John K. Cannon, commander of U.S. Air Forces in Europe, wrote that each wing and unit commander there saw the need for the new policy and was giving it fullest support; that there was some passive resentment among white airmen but few incidents; that reports from base commanders showed that the efficiency and personality of Negro officers assigned as fighter pilots, dentists, engineers or supply officers were "impressively good."

Edwards said the "word was passed around" throughout the Air Force that anyone opposing the new system could be honorably discharged upon request. It was not put in writing, he explained, since this might have led to misuse of the integration program as an excuse for otherwise-motivated resignations.

Letters from the commanders told of two or three departures. Of two white airmen at Sheppard Air Force Base, Texas, who balked at eating or sleeping with Negroes, one refused to re-enlist when his term of service was up; the other got used to integration "without further friction or resentment." A major at another base said that forcing white soldiers to eat, bathe and relax with men they did not welcome socially was carrying discipline into the field of politics; he resigned. But such cases were isolated.

Instances of overt resistance to the new policy were quickly stamped out, some with great severity. At Goodfellow Air Force Base, San Angelo, Texas, a white airman who insulted a Negro and challenged him to fight was court-martialed, sentenced to thirty days' confinement and then dismissed from the Air Force. An officer using the word "niggers" in addressing troops at Francis E. Warren Air Base, Cheyenne, Wyoming, was "advised" to apologize. In doing so, his insolent attitude further angered the Negroes. The officer was told in no uncertain terms how he must behave in the Air Force, and apparently liked his career well enough to pay heed.

One incident had a more plaintive character. A lone Negro airman at the Muroc, California, test base told an interviewer he was lonesome. The commander concerned wrote Edwards drily, "It is expected the assignment of additional colored personnel there will alleviate his complaint."

Besides fears of the reaction of white airmen, there was apprehension about communities near the many southern air bases. With extraordinary interest, therefore, Edwards read a letter from Keesler Field at Biloxi, Mississippi, heart of the deep South. Dated August 20, 1949, it related three incidents. A white airman had gone to the Negro section of town seeking a procurer to find a Negro woman. A Negro airman took two Negro girls to a white veterans' club to get liquor. Two airmen, a white and a Negro, tried to buy tickets together to a local theater; when they were turned away, the white airman called a policeman and began arguing about civil rights.

But the reporting officer said that the incidents had been handled without fanfare in routine fashion. The airman who wandered into forbidden Negro-town was fined fifteen dollars by local police for being drunk and disorderly, and reprimanded by his squadron leader. The white airman who argued about tickets likewise was fined. The two Negroes were freed by Biloxi police and returned to their base. There was no serious flare-up of local sentiment.

Air Force community racial problems were not limited to the South; in the West and Northwest, sparse Negro populations in nearby towns made off-the-base entertainment for Negro airmen a serious concern. The Chamber of Commerce of one northwestern city protested to the Air Force against plans to assign Negroes to a nearby air base, saying there had been a near riot of Negro soldiers there during World War II and that the city had few facilities to entertain Negro airmen.

The businessmen were told that the Air Force could not alter its plans. But when the Negroes arrived, the base commander formed them into choral groups and kept them busy after hours practicing Christmas carols; then he arranged for them to sing in the city's churches at Christmas. Thus the townspeople met the Negroes for the first time in church instead of outside saloons and complaints from that city died away.

Negro airmen used considerable restraint in entering military social circles before they were fully acceptable. Cannon in Europe reported that several commanders suggested to the Negroes that "undue forwardness" would be "disadvantageous." He said the Negroes "see the point and accept the counsel gratefully."

A Pentagon official visited one Texas air base and found the Negro airmen "flying" when whites brought their girls to swim in the pool. The white airmen stayed away when the Negroes brought their girls. There was no arbitrary ruling, this official reported, but a true gentlemen's agreement among men sensitive to southern feelings.

All was not compromise with southern customs. One commander at an air base in South Carolina removed a subordinate who refused to end separate Negro and white airmen's clubs, and put in an officer who erased the color line, with no untoward consequences.

The letters from the Air Force commanders, taken together, showed a significant conclusion — one that was reported independently by the Fahy Committee after visits to seven air bases in late 1949: that, despite sharply varying methods used to put over the new program, there was no appreciable difference in results.

The committee attributed this to "resolution of command," from Air Force headquarters in Washington down through local commanders. "Unquestionably, however," it added, "the almost total absence of opposition that had been anticipated in the enlisted men is a contributing factor in the success of the policy. The men were more ready for equality of treatment and opportunity than the officer corps had realized."

General Cannon, summing up progress in a letter to Edwards on January 3, 1950, said that six months' experience with integration in Europe had failed to produce a recorded instance of racial conflict, and he expected continued success. Negroes in the European Air Command, he said were above average intelligence, grateful for equal treatment and "extend themselves to do their full share of making it succeed"; whites "accept it or are generously tolerant."

"Complete acceptance of the Negro as a co-member," concluded Cannon, "depends on the Negro meeting the white man's concept of what a man should be."

The Air Force program was not entirely lacking in humor. The first Negro airman assigned to a rescue unit at Biggs Field, El Paso, Texas, called his flight commander from New York requesting permission to marry. Told he would have to report in first for "briefing," he phoned again the next day to say his intended bride had a child five years old and his future father-in-law was going to shoot him unless he married her at once. Permission was promptly granted.

"It is believed that the sergeant, with his newly acquired ready-made family, has not as yet reported to his organization," General Kuter wrote Edwards. "When he does, additional problems will be met on the same basis as those of a white airman. The solution was successful in that the commander concerned prevented his man from getting shot which, after all, is a considerable accomplishment tending toward a definite improvement of morale."

At the bottom of his letter Kuter noted, "A touch of levity may in fact be helpful in your business."

TWELVE

Korea Converts the Army

"In the Air Force an airman is an airman; in the Army a Negro is a Negro."

That statement, made by a high-ranking American officer in Austria in late 1949, mirrored the Army's basic policy on race at a time when the Air Force was rapidly tearing down its segregation barrier.

The Army was the mule of the military team on this issue. It had a vastly greater share of Negroes, both in numbers and percentage, and was more sensitive to pressure from southern politicians. Besides, certain men high in army councils opposed any change in the status quo, and bitterly resisted efforts to end segregation.

Following the Gillem Board's recommendations in 1946, a

number of Negroes had been given "housekeeping" jobs on Army posts, but they were largely concentrated in trucking, clerical and service work and for the most part lived in segregated quarters. Efforts to widen opportunities for Negroes were successfully resisted by certain officers within the army high command, according to documents in the Fahy Committee's files.

The Fahy Committee won Army Secretary Gordon Gray's agreement to open up progressively more specialist jobs to Negroes in all army units, and to remove the Army's quota on Negro inductions, though Gray obtained President Truman's secret written agreement to go back to a quota if the Army received a "disproportionate" number of Negroes.[1] Little had occurred under the new policy, announced in January, 1950, by the time the Korean War started on June 25 of that year.

There was, however, one significant development in 1949. Fort Ord, California, had been reactivated as an army training center when the draft was re-enacted and America, faced with growing Russian hostility, began to recoup her military strength. But in the Far West, Negroes were few and Negro inductees came into Ord slowly. Officers there discovered they might have training staffs of forty to sixty officers handling as few as eighteen or twenty Negroes if they maintained separate companies.

Colonel Harrison W. Pells, a New Englander, then Classification and Assignment Officer at Ord, said he concluded it would be simple common sense to put the Negroes and whites together. He discussed the question with his superiors, and Major General Robert T. Frederick, commander at Ord, approved the proposal. Officers assigned to Ord later said they arrived to find the integration working without a ripple.

[1]This document was shown to the author by a qualified source whom he is not at liberty to identify.

That appeared to be the first instance of integration of a major army unit in modern times. Army authorities in Washington seemed to have learned about it for the first time by way of a news clipping from a California newspaper. With their news policy in the process of evolving, they did nothing to stop the move; neither did they consider it a guide to future policy, because it was on a small scale and outside the South where they faced their chief problem.

A more far-reaching step came shortly after the outbreak of the Korean War. Fort Jackson, South Carolina, under orders to close in the spring of 1950, was reactivated as a major infantry training base. Brigadier General Frank McConnell was chosen to set up and command the 8th U.S. Infantry Division to train draftees.

He had been expected to set up a separate organization to train Negro inductees, and had received a special training "cadre" or staff of Negro and white officers and noncoms from Fort Dix, New Jersey, to handle the job.

The first draftees arrived in August. "I tried to sort them by color," McConnell said later, "but they began pouring in more rapidly; we got up to 1,000 recruits a day." Arriving without any pattern — busloads of Negroes, then busloads of whites — it was "totally impractical to sort them out."

McConnell conferred with his staff and proposed to put the Negroes and whites into platoons together. A staff member expressed fear McConnell might be going "off the deep end," suggesting a check with General Mark W. Clark, Chief of Army Field Forces.

"I pulled out the Army announcement on non-segregation," recounted McConnell. This was Gray's order of January, 1950. "It was all the authority I needed. I said that if we didn't ask permission, they couldn't stop us." However, he telephoned

Lieutenant General John R. Hodge, an old friend and commander of the Third Army which included Fort Jackson, and informed him on "about the same day; he was all for it, considered it the practical thing to do."

McConnell issued instructions that the next fifty-five draftees who arrived, regardless of color, would be formed into a platoon, and the same with subsequent arrivals. The order was issued verbally, he said, "and that was the end of segregation at Fort Jackson!"

He was not without concern about outside reaction, however, for Jackson was in the heart of the South. He conferred with G. A. Buchanan, Jr., editor of *The Record,* afternoon newspaper in nearby Columbia, South Carolina, who was also chairman of the Army Advisory Committee for Fort Jackson. Buchanan thought there would be no serious objection from civilians. McConnell asked him and the city's other newspaper not to publicize the new step, and they agreed.

The new program went into effect smoothly. There were no interracial incidents in the nine months McConnell was at Jackson. "I would see recruits, Negro and white, walking down the street, all buddying together; the attitude of the Southern soldiers was that this was the army way; they accepted it the same way they accepted getting booted out of bed at 5:30 in the morning."

Soon, said McConnell, word of the "new look" at Jackson began to get around. The Army sent Major Steve Davis, a Negro general staff officer, down from Washington and he was very enthusiastic. In the fall McConnell discussed his integration program with General Clark; "he saw them all mixed up, and he was quite in favor of it." Clark and Hodge were so enthusiastic about the resulting speed-up in training, added McConnell, that commanders and staffs of every training division in the United States were ordered to visit Fort Jackson and observe. Soon integration was proceeding rapidly at all ten training bases.

McConnell recalled that he received a visit from a prominent Columbia, South Carolina, businessman whose son was under his command. The father said that a Negro soldier in his son's squad slept in the lower half of his double-decker bunk. Both were from Columbia. His son accepted it as the Army way and they got along fine, though the Negro offered to wake up his white squadmate in the morning and shine his shoes.

In Korea, meanwhile, a battlefield test of the new army racial experiment was in the making.

Colonel John G. Hill was in command of the 9th U.S. Infantry Regiment, one of the first U.S. contingents to land in July, 1950, while the North Koreans were still pushing southward in their first great offensive. He had 10 percent overstrength in his all-Negro 3rd Battalion, and his two white battalions were short of men. Battle losses swiftly cut deeper into his white units.

As Hill related it, "force of circumstances" induced him to shift his excess Negroes to the white battalions. "We had no replacements. We had to use untrained South Korean contingents. We would have been doing ourselves a disservice to permit [Negro] soldiers to lie around in rear areas at the expense of the still further weakening of our [white] rifle companies."

No sooner were the Negroes integrated in the white battalions, continued Hill, than they became better soldiers. "They even volunteered to go on night patrols." One six-foot-five, 200-pound Negro offered to carry a bulky radio on a night patrol across the Naktong River. The patrol leader, asked if the Negro could go, replied, "Hell, yes! We re tickled to death to have him."

Hill said he knew the Negroes would be accepted in white units "because at a time like that, misery loves company." He added that there was "not one manifestation of disfavor." Hill informed Major General Laurence B. Keiser, commander of the U.S. 2nd Division, of his action and Keiser heartily approved.

One of officers with the 2nd Division at the time, who accompanied it during its bloody retreat from the Yalu River in November, 1950, was Brigadier General S. L. A. Marshall, noted military historian then serving as Infantry Operations Analyst for the U.S. Eighth Army in Korea.

Marshall said later it was during this retreat that he first encountered integrated units. He said they were not only good, but several fought "brilliantly." One Texas colonel, commanding the most thoroughly integrated battalion in the 2nd Division, "would fight anybody who even inferred that his troops were not as good as anybody else's," Marshall recalled.

On December 18, in a two-hour oral report on the Yalu disaster to Lieutenant General Walton H. Walker, Eighth Army Commander, and his staff, Marshall reported among other things that racial integration had proved itself.

He said that General Walker, who was later killed in a jeep accident in Korea, was "extremely interested" and asked him to make the same statement to the press the next day. This Marshall did, only to receive prompt word that General Douglas MacArthur's headquarters took an extremely dim view of the racial mixing.

Deeply disturbed, Marshall flew to MacArthur's United Nations Command Headquarters in Tokyo. There he found a "completely negative view" toward what he felt had proved a valuable new development in Army treatment of Negro troops.

He pleaded with a high official on MacArthur's staff at least to order further study, to interview commanders and question white men who had served alongside Negroes. His request was rejected.

The official to whom Marshall talked felt Negroes could never become successful fighters. Marshall was also told, courteously but firmly, that the Army would not become the "guinea pig" for social change.

Marshall did not talk to MacArthur directly on this subject. However, Pentagon officials said that MacArthur showed no interest in integration of Negro and white troops, which got its major impetus in Korea when General Matthew B. Ridgway replaced MacArthur as U. N. and U. S. commander.

Meanwhile, Lieutenant General Edward M. Almond, still bitter from his unhappy World War II experience with the all-Negro 92nd Division in Italy, after a hitch as MacArthur's Chief of Staff, arrived in Korea in January to head the U.S. 10th Corps, which included the partly integrated 2nd Division.

Major General Clark L. Ruffner, assuming command of the 2nd Division at the same time, said he found Negroes mingled among white battalions and they "seemed to be doing all right; I saw a lot of [Negro] men with silver stars; I never got any complaints."

But Almond was shocked to find Negroes in white combat battalions. He ordered Ruffner to find out exactly how it had come about. Almond also swiftly set about to reverse the process.

"We just didn't replace Negroes in white units when they left by attrition," explained Ruffner. "We got it almost back to where it was — all-white and all-Negro battalions — under Almond's directives."

Then came a large shipment of Negro replacements. Ruffner said there were far too many to put in the division's two all-

Negro battalions. He wanted to assign some to white combat artillery, but was under strict orders from Almond not to place Negroes in white combat outfits.

"So I integrated them into white combat-service units — engineers, quartermasters, and so on," said Ruffner. "I took them into my own headquarters, integrated them completely. I had to — I had all those men and had to do something with them."

They did a "damn fine job," he added; there never was any trouble from southern whites, nor any Negro-white conflict. Members of Ruffner's staff recalled that he was privately furious with Almond for not permitting use of Negroes in white combat battalions, considering this refusal to have caused a serious waste of manpower.

Meanwhile, a situation was building up in the United States which, according to a competent authority, was verging on a national scandal. Because of the army policy of using Negro troops predominantly behind the lines, Negro army strength was piling up at home; it had reached 23 percent of total army strength in the United States in the spring of 1951.

Earl D. Johnson, then Assistant Army Secretary for manpower, warned against the growing concentration which already had led to lowered efficiency and increased A.W.O.L. and venereal disease rates among Negro troops.

Johnson also talked quietly to southern lawmakers, emphasizing that whites were taking more than their share of casualties in Korea.

One other major factor gave impetus to the emerging plan for an all-out racial shift in Korea — the Army's conclusion that the all-Negro 24th Infantry Regiment was unreliable in combat, and a recommendation by a high-ranking army commander in Korea that it be broken up; the commander emphasized he was criticizing the regiment as a unit, not the individual Negro soldiers.

General Ridgway, who replaced MacArthur as Far Eastern Commander and who had witnessed the successful integration "experiments," asked the Defense Department for permission to integrate all Negroes throughout his command. He was authorized to go ahead. Between May and August, the extent of integration in Korea jumped from 9 to 30 percent of troops in the field.

On July 21, 1951, the public was cautiously invited to share the Army's long-kept secret. A carefully worded press release said that the Army was breaking up the all-Negro 24th Infantry Regiment and was integrating Negroes and whites throughout its Far Eastern Command.

The Army scrutinized press reaction anxiously. With few exceptions, the move was enthusiastically received. *The New York Times* said the sooner all military segregation was ended, the better. The chief critic was the Communist *Daily Worker,* which scoffed at the move as a "backhanded slap at Negro soldiers"; it said "no sincere fighter against Jim Crow is going to be fooled into thinking J. C. is going to be killed by disbanding one all-Negro regiment."

The Charleston, South Carolina *News and Courier,* one of the few southern papers to comment editorially, said nobody had suggested that the Negro should be considered unfit to fight and die for his country; but it added that mixing races in the armed forces "may have far-reaching social consequences, the extent of which we are not now prepared to say."

"But, as FDR used to say," it concluded, "we are on our way."

THIRTEEN

Trial by Fire

In the summer of 1951, after ordering racial integration in Korea, the Army began a new and highly secret operation. Labeled "Project Clear," it involved sending teams of trained interviewers to Korea, and to training bases in the United States, to examine the new racial policy under the social scientist's microscope.*

The Navy and Air Force had tried non-segregation, found that it worked and let it go at that. The larger and more cautious Army wanted the best available assessors to test the

---

*The author was given access to the findings of "Project Clear" while doing research for the book on condition that he not name the source of the study. Since that time, the then "Secret" study has been declassified and can be identified as having been conducted in 1951 by the Operations Research Office of Johns Hopkins University.

new structure before putting its full weight on it. The conclusions of the researchers, staff workers of three university and civilian research agencies, under joint supervision and operating under contract to the Army, fill three thick volumes and constitute some of the most important racial findings of this century. They reach beyond the military sphere and provide clues to what the military experiment may mean to the future of race relations in America.

The principal question for the Army was: How do Negro soldiers perform in combat? Working close to the battle line, the interviewers handed questionnaires to 245 battalion and company officers with one or more months of experience with racially mixed units.

Of 185 officers who completed the forms, majorities of 66 to 90 percent rated Negroes in mixed units "about on a par" with white soldiers on nearly every one of twenty-eight aspects of combat behavior!

On the crucial test of standing up to mass attack, where Negro soldiers in the past had sometimes broken and run, 85 percent of the officers found Negroes in mixed units performed "about the same" as white soldiers.

In care of weapons, another important phase of soldiering in which Negroes had been criticized, 90 percent found "integrated" Negroes were on a par with whites.

Eighty-eight percent of those questioned said that Negro officers of integrated units led their men by personal example and stayed with them in combat to an equal extent with white leaders. Over two-thirds believed that a hazardous mission would succeed equally well if led by a Negro as by a white.

Reports from the fighting line backed up these opinions. Brigadier General S. L. A. Marshall, in his book, *The River and the Gauntlet,* described the stark heroism of Lieutenant Ellison

C. Wynn, a Negro officer in Baker Company of the integrated 9th Infantry Regiment, during the retreat of the Eighth Army from the Yalu River in November, 1950. Ordered to take command of a mortar position, Wynn led his men in a night of bitter fighting during which the Chinese Communists surrounded Baker Company. At last, ammunition gone and half his men dead or wounded, he ordered the rest to run, shouting that he would cover them.

As the men prepared to flee, they saw Wynn, weaponless, bend over and come up with an armload of rocks and canned C-rations. These he hurled at the Chinese with such ferocity that the startled Chinese slackened their fire, enabling most of the men to escape. The Chinese soon resumed their attack; Wynn, one side of his face blown away by a grenade, managed to stagger down the hill to another position where he continued to direct his men, refusing bandages and morphine until he fainted from loss of blood. He spent 117 days in the hospital and recovered, receiving the Distinguished Service Cross for his action.

One testing technique is to approach a problem from different angles. A second team of interviewers in Korea quizzed another group of 200 white officers on unfavorable incidents involving Negro and white soldiers in racially mixed units.

These officers, asked to list instances of specified types of adverse conduct, reported more cases of running away, poor care of equipment, and laziness among Negroes than among whites; but *fewer* examples of malingering, refusal to move forward and poor leadership among Negroes. The officers did not rate any of the differences sharp enough to detract from the fighting quality of racially mixed units, which they agreed overwhelmingly were effective.

Next the survey teams turned to the men themselves, questioning them on the performance of their squadmates with no mention of race. Questionnaires were handed to 1,563 white and 221 Negro members of integrated rifle squads, scattered among eight regiments in four different divisions. The men were asked to record specific instances they had witnessed of six types of behavior — good and bad — on the part of their squadmates: good morale under stress, courage and aggressiveness, judgment and skill; and their opposites, poor morale, lack of courage, and poor judgment.

The white soldiers reported observing slightly more instances of good morale, courage and judgment among whites than Negroes; an equal frequency of occasions on which both Negro and white squadmates displayed lack of courage and poor judgment; and they recalled slightly *fewer* specific illustrations of poor morale among Negroes.

Negro soldiers gave very slightly higher rating to Negroes than did whites.

The researchers concluded that Negroes in integrated squads, as rated by their Negro and white squadmates, showed "substantially the same frequencies of desirable and undesirable combat behavior" as white soldiers; "the similarities far outweigh the differences."

Turning to the United States, the researchers found that the farther away from experience with integration the less favorable the reaction.

Summing up their findings in Korea and the United States, the social scientists concluded that a large majority of both officers and enlisted men with experience in integrated units found them just about equal to all-white units. Significantly they found that 11 to 15 percent of officers and men with integration knowledge rated mixed units *superior in morale* to white units! Some reasons will be suggested later.

Why, asked the researchers, did Negro soldiers perform erratically or badly in all-Negro outfits and well in mixed units? For one thing, they discovered Negro units were often torn by inner conflict. "Hell, we fight all the time," a Negro soldier told them.

Negroes in segregated units felt they were set apart and despised. As a Negro infantryman expressed it, "If the army is going to be like it is now (his unit was still segregated), the morale of my race will be very low. I think some of my pals feel that we are in a different army than the white troops by the way we are treated."

But after integration, interviews with both white and Negro soldiers showed that, in a mixed unit, the Negro acquired a new sense of pride and self-respect, and no longer saw himself as a second-class citizen and soldier. He knew his opportunities and treatment were the same as white troops', and his ambitions might be stirred by the challenge of competing with white soldiers whose standards were usually higher.

Explained one Negro infantryman to the army interviewers: "The Negro feels like he is letting his race down if he is thrown in with a bunch of whites and proves to be the ass end of everything that goes on. He concentrates on being a good fellow and a regular fellow. He begins to see the fellows getting along in the Army and begins to say to himself, it would be so goddam nice if it could be like that all over. You begin to forget about being colored and want to make your company or battalion the best outfit of the post."

A few Negroes were found who preferred segregation, such as one who told the interviewers, "I prefer a segregated unit; you can't talk business with someone you don't know good." But those questioned overwhelmingly favored integration. The researchers came to the conclusion: Negroes in all-Negro organizations *"do* often exhibit the failings charged to them; in integrated units they tend to approach the average performance level and no longer represent a problem."

They followed with an illuminating observation: "The forces of competition that cause the Negro to improve his performance may also spur the efforts of the whites" — a possible bonus from integration that may explain reports of higher morale among mixed units.

Moving on to personal interviews with senior officers in integrated units in the United States, the army research teams found a "consistent pattern": those who believed integration would work *reaffirmed their judgment on the basis of experience;* those who did not think so previously reported *that experience had changed their opinion.*

The opinion-finders said such judgments were as common among southern officers as northerners, southerners frequently calling attention to their home states to emphasize the extent of their conversion.

"I'm a Texan and I suppose I was as anti-Negro as the next Texan before I got acquainted with integration a few years back," said one regiment commander. "But I can truthfully say I'm sold on it now."

Throughout all the interviews the element of surprise at the success of integration ran like a continuous thread. "I'm very surprised," the researchers quoted one captain as saying. "I would have bet my bottom dollar it wouldn't work."

Officers expressing adverse reactions were a very small minority; some white officers believed integration improved Negro efficiency at the expense of white effectiveness, and that even under the best conditions Negro performance was below that of the whites.

All right, said the researchers. We've found that integration gives Negroes new pride and a will to do their part, and does not materially lower the efficiency of white units. But aren't the Negroes resented? Is the Army sitting on a keg of dynamite?

The answer was typified by a division chief of staff, who said he had been skeptical when integration was ordered in his division. "My officers told me we'd have riots, murder, low standards of training, conflict with the state law, trouble with the townspeople, etc," he said. "But we didn't. We haven't had any trouble and we won't have."

The researchers reported that they made a *persistent search* for evidence of trouble, or even prospects of trouble, using additional questionnaire techniques to find out if GI's thought integration would lead to friction or conflict. The answers were overwhelmingly in the negative. In fact, they reported integration seemed to *lessen* racial tension rather than increase it. The few instances of racial tension reported, they said, were generally in *segregated* garrison units in Japan and the United States — and then mostly off the post.

The researchers further reported that intimate contacts of military life broke down traditional white "stereotypes" or fixed ideas about Negroes, and associations and friendships sprang up. Of 1,730 white trainees in mixed units in the United States, 19 percent reported spending off-duty time with Negroes both on and off the post. Fifty-nine percent of the Negroes reported similar association with whites. One survey team recorded an interview with a Negro trainee who said he, three other Negroes and one white soldier were sitting around one night when suddenly the white man spoke.

"Not meaning any offense, but before I came in the Army I didn't know how you all were. I didn't know how it would be. Now I can see you're just like anybody else and I'm glad we all got together this way. We've had no fights or arguments. I thought before, with the way you all are treated back home and all, you probably might not like being with us."

The Negro said, "I explained it to him, how we understands lots of things about this before he does, because we have to come up from the bottom so we see how it is all the way up."

"Funny," the Negro added, "he thought we'd be embarrassed by him saying that."

Still another study by a new army research group discovered there was almost no objection to military integration from people in nearby towns and cities, even at bases in the southern part of the United States. Local residents took the attitude that the Army could do what it pleased, as long as it did not interfere with local ways.

In their final summation, the combined groups of social scientists said that the United States had "inadequate" manpower reserves to meet possible mobilization demands; that the 15,000,000 U.S. Negroes were a vital part of the manpower pool for present and future military needs; and that the militarily fit portion of this critical one-tenth of the nation could not be utilized to full effectiveness except in *integrated* military organizations.

On November 1, 1951, the experts delivered their voluminous report to the Army. Their findings were conclusive: integration of Negroes meant an overall gain for the Army, and would cause no serious trouble either within the Army or with nearby communities. They recommended pushing rapidly ahead to complete integration of the entire Army.

The Army was ready for its final breakthrough on the color front.

FOURTEEN

A Soldier Is a Soldier

To the people of Austria, still occupied by Russian and Western troops in 1951, some Soviet propaganda made sense. Communist speakers sneered, "The Americans preach equality; yet Negroes among U.S. occupation troops are kept in subjugation."

In the Pentagon in Washington, Lieutenant General Stafford L. "Red" Irwin, chief of the Army's "G-2" Intelligence division, saw daily dispatches showing how Russia was making propaganda capital of segregation. Sent to Austria to command U.S. occupation troops, he found himself on the receiving end of that propaganda.

Irwin figured the most direct answer was to remove the target of the attack. Army Secretary Frank C. Pace, Jr., in

Europe during the summer of 1951, visited Irwin, who told him, "I want to integrate." Pace returned to Washington and conferred with Earl Johnson, his Assistant Secretary for manpower. They agreed to let Irwin go ahead.

It was done very quietly. Lieutenant General Anthony C. McAuliffe, then Deputy Chief of Staff for Personnel, confessed later he himself did not even know Irwin had acted until white artillery replacements were scheduled for Austria and Irwin wired urgently not to send them — he was "integrated."

Austria became an integrated patch in the overall segregated pattern of army forces in Europe. General Thomas C. Handy, a Virginian in command of U.S. Army troops in Europe, was dubious about the new experiment.

In June, 1951, with Korean integration actively under way, Earl Johnson sent Dr. Eli Ginzberg, Columbia University professor and army consultant on manpower, to Europe to pave the way for ending segregation there. At European Command headquarters in Heidelberg, Germany, Ginzberg told Handy's staff the Army was interested in considering racial integration in their theater.

They were absolutely in favor of it, they told Ginzberg, but added it would take fifty to 100 years. Many were flatly opposed to such a radical step — a reflection, Ginzberg felt, of Handy's views.

From Heidelberg, Ginzberg went to Stuttgart to visit Lieutenant General Manton S. Eddy, then commanding the U.S. Seventh Army. When Ginzberg told Eddy about the Army's desire for integration, he said Eddy "almost fell on my neck." Eddy had units he considered "absolutely unreliable" because of segregation, and said integration would be the greatest possible aid to success of his training program.

Korean integration was now an established fact and the army

research teams had logged it incomparably superior to the old segregated system. But Handy and his staff argued that the Korean experience did not apply to Europe. They said theirs was an occupation army in which social relationships were more important than in Korea.

By this time, however, the Army was in the full tide of the new movement. Army officials in a position to know said that Pace and General J. Lawton Collins, Army Chief of Staff, asked Handy to submit to Washington his plan for integration in Europe, knowing Handy had no such plan. Seeing the handwriting on the wall, he made haste to draw one up and rushed it to the Pentagon.

Integration specialists in General McAuliffe's personnel branch found Handy's program generally good. They made some changes, knocking out Handy's suggestions for sending home all Negroes who fell below a certain mental standard, and for reducing the number of Negro officers likely to command whites. McAuliffe explained later, "the treatment had to be identical."

Collins, in a personal letter to Handy, then "approved" Handy's revised plan. Handy, apparently determined not to have the record show he was starting integration voluntarily, issued an order on April 1, 1952, stating, "The Department of the Army has directed this command to initiate a . . . program of racial integration. . . ."

Without fixing a firm deadline, the plan provided generally for complete integration of combat units within six months to one year, and of service units in one to two years.

It wasn't long before Handy and the men around him changed their attitude toward the non-segregation program. Ginzberg, who visited the European theater in 1952, said that the same staff officers who previously told him integration

116

would take fifty to 100 years now tried to convince *him* it would work then and there.

The European program went forward under Handy, and even more swiftly when General Eddy moved into Handy's job in the summer of 1952. A Negro major wrote to friends in the Pentagon in October, 1952, that integration was "going much more rapidly than the plan envisaged; all our officers are doing exceptionally well and there have been no race incidents; I believe the general consensus is that they didn't know we had it in us; all of us should do well under the integrated setup, and I think our futures are assured if we continue to do our jobs."

Ernest Leiser, writing in the *Saturday Evening Post* for December 13, 1952, told of the 272nd Field Artillery Battalion, an "eight-ball" Negro National Guard battalion with a miserable efficiency rating and an artillery firing record that was "one of the lowest in the command." He said morale and discipline reached a low ebb in January, 1952, when two German girls in the town where it was stationed were raped by unidentified Negro soldiers.

In mid-April came the order which sent 80 percent of the battalion's Negroes home or to other units, and brought in 80 percent white replacements. Lieutenant Colonel Jack S. Blocker, a southerner who commanded the 272nd, told the remaining Negroes that this was what they wanted for a long time: "Whether it works or is a monumental foul-up is going to depend very considerably on you — your qualities of leadership, your patience, how hard you work."

According to Leiser, the "new 272nd smartened up and straightened out almost immediately. Its incident [misbehavior] rate dropped, its efficiency rating rose. By the time it had shaken down in maneuvers near the Soviet-zone frontier, it had established its position as a competent, reliable outfit."

A Negro lieutenant explained why to Leiser. "He's [the Negro soldier] got a reason for trying now. He's not just competing against another Negro, knowing no matter how good he is no one will much care. He's not even competing against a white man. But he is competing against the standards of America, same as anyone else."

Assistant Secretary of the Army Fred Korth, who toured army bases in Europe late in 1952, reported on November 26th that combat effectiveness of U.S. forces in Europe and Austria had increased and that "the incident rate, A.W.O.L. rate and V.D. rate of all commands have steadily declined since integration began."

He described the reaction of both Negroes and whites as "generally good," and added that the "most important remedy" in handling problems that arose "has been a sympathetic understanding by the command, which is now quite evident both in USFA (Austria) and USAREUR (Europe)."

"Generally speaking, I think I can say quite confidently that our Negro program is proceeding very well in Europe, and that we are achieving benefits therefrom substantially greater than we had anticipated at its inception," Korth concluded.

The Army's European program was put into effect with no publicity; so was the final stage of integration within the United States.

Negro units of the six army commands in the continental United States and of the Alaskan command were plagued with a mounting overstrength problem throughout 1951. Commanders of Negro battalions supposed to contain 400 men found themselves with more than twice that number. Lacking enough officers and with men literally falling over each other, the commanders complained bitterly to their superiors.

Soon, from Alaska and from the Sixth Army in California,

which included already integrated Fort Ord, came urgent appeals saying in effect: "Let us integrate, or we'll do it anyway." Fort Eustis, Virginia, under Brigadier General Harold R. Duffie, integrated without waiting for a go-ahead.

A high-ranking army officer in the Pentagon, in a penciled note to General McAuliffe, said that local commanders were "forcing" the Army into final integration.

At length, verbal instructions were issued to a conference of U.S. and Alaskan army commanders in the Pentagon in December, 1951. Three steps were called for:

1. Integration of Negroes with whites in regular army divisions, to take about three months. When the 82nd Airborne Division at Fort Bragg, North Carolina, had not completed integration after six months, an officer from Washington was sent to hurry it up.
2. Non-divisional units were to receive some of the excess Negro personnel from regular army battalions.
3. Negroes were to be taken out of any remaining all-Negro units and spread among other units.

McAuliffe was a strong advocate of letting local commanders work out their integration problems. Here is how that approach worked with the "lily white" 31st Division, a former Mississippi National Guard unit whose commander, Major General Alexander G. Paxton, swore he would never permit a Negro in his outfit.

Paxton was due to retire in the fall of 1952. "We'll just wait until he does," McAuliffe told this writer in the summer of that year. When Paxton retired that autumn, Major General Harry J. "Lighthorse Harry" Collins was given command of the 31st. Collins had succeeded General McConnell as commander at Fort Jackson and was favorable to the new non-segregation policy. By the spring of 1953, Negro replacements had been sifted into the 31st without noticeable difficulty.

Another milestone in the military's quiet revolution had been passed without a shot fired or a trumpet sounded.

FIFTEEN

Silence and the Politicians

From the start of concrete planning to end segregation in the armed forces, until somewhere around 1952, military officials — particularly in the Army — maintained an almost complete curtain of secrecy around their actions. It could well have been called "Operation Hush-Hush."

Army public information officers, who were completely cooperative in digging out the full story of integration in 1952-53, said there was no outright ban on news of early nonsegregation steps. But as late as mid-1952 this author, asking about the extent of army integration, was told by an official *who had the precise data* that no such information was available.

"We agreed there would be no publicity," a senior army general staff officer explained later. "We were afraid that if

120

there were a lot of stories in the papers, southern congressmen would have to get up on their hind legs and oppose it. We wanted to get it done without fanfare — then tell about it."

This dovetailed with the view of influential members of Congress. Leading officials of the Army and Air Force discussed their integration plans in advance — and in secret — with key members of the Senate and House Armed Services Committees, laying heavy stress on their belief that integration would improve military efficiency. Some military leaders also emphasized to southern legislators that failure to use Negroes equally in combat would mean extra-heavy white losses, leaving a growing percentage of Negroes at home in local communities. The southerners understood the implication.

An Air Force official said he got the impression the committees were "skeptical but wouldn't interfere as long as it was in the interest of efficiency and there was no noise about it."

One of the most powerful southern senators, asked by this writer why he did not publicly fight the Air Force and army integration programs, said; "I could have got up and shouted, and the home folks would have said, 'Hooray, there's ———— ———— up there raising hell,' but it might only have made things more difficult for the military and it wouldn't have changed anything."

This senator said Kenneth C. Royall, Army Secretary in 1947 and 1948, promised that the Army would not do anything "precipitate" toward ending segregation, and the promise was adhered to until the Korean War. But with the war came casualties and an urgent need for more fighting manpower. The senator said General J. Lawton Collins, Army Chief of Staff, told him in 1951 that the all-Negro outfits in Korea were unsatisfactory, and the Army was going to have to integrate them with white units because it desperately needed replacements.

"I didn't object," the southerner said. "He already knew how I felt, and besides it wouldn't have done any good."

Whatever the reasons for the silence of the southerners, military leaders were thankful; they feared that public controversy, if started, might reach into communities near military posts or the ranks of GI's themselves and stir up the very dissension and riots so many feared would result from integration.

Northern congressmen favoring non-segregation joined in the conspiracy of silence. Senator Hubert H. Humphrey of Minnesota, one of the most outspoken Democrats on civil rights issues, said he arranged a conference with army leaders when a Minnesota delegation complained to him about segregated conditions forced on unsegregated Minnesota National Guard troops sent to Camp Rucker, Alabama. Humphrey told the army officials that Minnesota had tried for seventy-five years to establish a non-segregated society and did not intend to have the government force a reversal of its progress. He said he was speaking for other Democratic senators: Paul H. Douglas of Illinois, Herbert H. Lehman of New York, William H. Benton of Connecticut, Harley M. Kilgore and Matthew M. Neely of West Virginia, Warren G. Magnuson of Washington and John Pastore of Rhode Island. He told the military officials, "You've got to decide who you want trouble with, the southerners or us."

Humphrey related that he and his colleagues agreed to keep quiet about the issue as long as the military kept its promise to report progress, though he added that his political opponents in Minnesota clamored that he was doing nothing about army segregation.

The military's own close-mouthed policy helped keep the

news out of the headlines. The Army's silence was broken for the first time by a brief, carefully worded announcement in July, 1951, that integration of all army units in the Far Eastern Theater was under way. General staff officers discussed their Korean plan long in advance with army public information specialists. The specialists urged holding off the breakup of the Negro 24th Infantry Regiment until the Army could announce integration throughout the entire Far Eastern Command; this would present *positive* news along with the *negative.* Their advice was followed.

The final press release withheld praise or blame of the Negro regiment, avoided any crusading language, stating simply that the Negro unit would be disbanded and Negroes integrated throughout the Far Eastern Command in the interest of military efficiency.

The generals waited anxiously for the reaction and were astonished at its paucity; almost all was favorable, except for the sneers of the Communist *Daily Worker* in New York City. The social science researchers who studied the army integration program made a special survey of press reaction to the Far East integration announcement, and concluded that the favorable reaction was a "direct reflection" of the way the Army handled the publicity.

After that the Army clammed up again. It ordered overall integration in Europe and throughout continental United States, but did not announce it. Only months after these additional steps were under way did word begin to filter into newspapers; the full impact of the Army's actions did not become generally known until the end of 1953.

Even that late, there were military men who felt it was still unwise to publicize the integration program, successful as it might be. One such officer, asked for information about the

124

integrated elementary school at Fort Bragg, North Carolina, replied, "It's working so well I don't want anything said about it. It might upset the applecart. Remember you're in North Carolina. Let's don't ruffle the hair of Cumberland County."

One of the quietest of the Army's operations was the repeal of the old laws establishing the four all-Negro regiments. The laws had been cited in the past as an argument for maintaining segregation. In 1950, without publicity, they were repealed by *statute number* in a catch-all bill canceling several other "outmoded" military acts. No mention could be found in Senate or House committee hearings that the Negro regiments were involved; the legal basis for them simply vanished without a trace.

Subsequently the 9th and 10th Cavalry Regiments, famed in Indian fighting and Spanish-American War days, were converted into the 509th and 510th Negro Tank Battalions on October 20, 1950, and integrated with white units on March 7, 1953, and December 31, 1952, respectively.

The 24th Infantry Regiment, its members already spread among white units in Korea, was officially inactivated on October 1, 1951. The 25th Infantry Regiment was broken up into three Negro battalions on October 20, 1950; two of these, the 94th and 95th Infantry Battalions, were inactivated December 20 and 22, 1952, respectively; the third, the 25th Infantry Battalion, was redesignated the 25th Armored Infantry Battalion on March 20, 1951, and became integrated as an organic unit of the 1st Armored Division on November 20, 1952.

Methods for overcoming or bypassing opposition to integration were sometimes devious. One border state delegation in Congress, faced with strong opposition to non-segregation from groups back home, made a "deal" with the Army not to integrate a unit from their state, then in Japan, until it got to Korea; once in combat the unit was integrated and the congressmen explained to the objectors it was a battlefield necessity.

Integration advocates played one service against another. The Navy's ice-breaking non-segregation program was cited repeatedly in arguments with the Army and Air Force as evidence that integration would work. Then Air Force integration was added to the navy experience as a lever on the Army. In 1953, foes of segregation were pointing to the nearly complete army integration as well as the Air Force achievement as arguments to push the Navy into integrating its Steward's Branch and eliminating other segregation practices.

Non-segregation as a principle, however, apparently was a fixed rule in the services by 1953 and no force, physical or political, seemed likely to change it. This could perhaps best be seen in statements of southern members of Senate and House Armed Services Committees. One highly respected House committee member, a southerner, said that public acceptance of military integration, even in the South, was shown by the fact that southern congressmen received almost no complaints about it any more.

"It's working," he said. "I don't know about the social aspects. The change must come about gradually. If the individual Negro has ability, he will win recognition.

"But for Heaven's sake, don't use my name."

Another member of the House Armed Services Committee, Representative O. C. Fisher, a Texas Democrat, did not object to being quoted directly.

"I'm not as exercised as some," he said. "I prefer segregation myself; but it's inevitable, because of government policies, that we're going to have a certain amount of integration. I had hoped they would respect the preferences of the men, but we haven't had a great deal of complaints."

Fisher said reports to the committee showed integration was preferable on the battlefield to segregation. "The military are better judges than we," he concluded. "It's working in Korea. The generals ought to know."

One of the most influential southerners on the Senate Armed Services Committee agreed that nearly all military authorities reported the integration program to be successful in combat. He said he had "no doubt at all" it would improve the overall United States fighting machine by increasing the usefulness of Negroes. He said he still received a few complaints from southern white servicemen who objected to sleeping and eating with Negroes, but nothing to compare with the "couple of hundred" letters he received when the Air Force non-segregation program went into effect in 1949.

This senator was convinced, when interviewed in August of 1953, that America's military establishment will never go back to segregation. It would be impossible to restore segregation with the political situation the way it is, he said. He emphasized that he himself still felt it wrong to compel white men to serve and live alongside Negroes if they did not want to, and expressed conviction that the armed forces could permit freedom of choice if they so desired.

This southerner said the chief reason behind his objection to all anti-segregation moves was his conviction that they would lead eventually to an "amalgamation of races — a brown race in America." Stating that he was undoubtedly "prejudiced" by his southern background, he felt nevertheless that such a development would be bad for the country.

"But it's bound to come," he added. 'You can't stop it."

This feeling of inevitability may explain why a Tennessee

mother, protesting to her congressman because her son was forced to sleep with Negroes in the Air Force, had no effect on the Air Force integration program.

The great French humanist, Victor Hugo, put it this way: "There is one thing stronger than all the armies in the world, and that is an idea whose time has come."

SIXTEEN

The Military Scene — 1953

From the start of the Korean War, military bases from coast to coast boomed with renewed activity as the United States trained a three and a half million man force for combat in Korea and readiness for any fresh Communist aggression.

Visits of this writer to seven bases during the year preceding the Korean armistice confirmed that the wall of racial segregation was almost gone. Here and there an individual or group of Negroes butted against a rampart, and mistakenly thought the barrier still intact. But numerous interviews with officers and men — Negroes and whites, commanders and privates — and personal observations in widely scattered parts of the country made it clear that the military's racial breakthrough was an accomplished fact.

Here, in capsule form, is a report on those visits, reproduced from voluminous notes and adding this author's personal findings to the military's own documentation of its successful racial revolution:

FORT JACKSON, SOUTH CAROLINA

Columbia, South Carolina, was the state capital of Governor James F. Byrnes, a leader in the South's battle to retain segregation. Yet at nearby Fort Jackson, where some 25,000 American youths were undergoing the rugged, sixteen-week course that makes a soldier, GI's were training, eating, sleeping and swimming together without racial distinction. On entering the gate one immediately became aware of the lack of segregation. On every hand, Negroes could be seen scattered among white soldiers in marching columns, or idling alongside whites around long, rectangular barracks buildings.

"Once a Negro gets inside the gate he is treated exactly like a white soldier," explained the base public information officer, Lieutenant Colonel Dwight Bingham. "He is a soldier, period." He added that southerners showed no concern when an instructor was a Negro, as long as the teacher knew his subject.

Major General Whitfield P. Shepard, from Syracuse, New York, base commander, sat stiffly at his desk. "There are no problems," he said. "It's working. We are obeying orders to effect integration." He declined to comment further.

The deputy post commander, Colonel Vachel D. Watley, Jr., was more willing to talk. He said it was inefficient not to integrate; "separate facilities are burdensome."

Lieutenant Colonel Franklin W. Patten, Assistant Chief of Staff for personnel, a North Dakotan, said that racial integration was working so well the subject never came up any more.

The lieutenant in charge of one 220-man company, 128 of them Negroes, considered it "satisfactory" to train Negroes and whites together; but he said later over a beer in the clubhouse that he would not want to go into combat with a mixed unit. The lieutenant, a South Carolinian and recent college graduate scheduled to leave soon for his first combat assignment, said white trainees did not like sleeping next to Negroes and "I wouldn't either." He said Negroes and whites remained aloof the first few days in camp, but "I tell them, none of you are black S.O.B.'s, none of you are white S.O.B.'s; you're going over there to fight together and you're going to get along!"

In the company barracks, busily cleaning their rifles, Negroes from Mississippi and Arkansas sat on double-decker bunks among whites from Georgia and South Carolina with no apparent antipathy.

A white draftee from Alabama said integration would be all right if barracks for Negroes were separate; he didn't mind working with them. A white soldier from Athens, Georgia, said he had not been accustomed to mixing with Negroes but was getting used to the idea; he felt he would be "just as confident" going into battle with them as with white soldiers alone. A white corporal from Hagerstown, Maryland, did not like Negroes in the Army, and said some of the southerners were "ready to pull out." He added, however, that two Negroes in his barracks, one with two years of college, were "real good; they're clean; I have no objection to *them.*"

Negroes almost without exception liked the new system. A Negro draftee from Mississippi, at Jackson for four months, said, "I like it here pretty good; I've had no trouble; I get along okay with the white boys and the other fellows [Negroes] feel the same way."

At enlisted men's "Club Number One," two noncoms from

Tennessee and Virginia, in charge of activities, said they had been "surprised as hell" to find mixed races at Jackson but didn't mind it any more. They explained that theirs was a predominantly "white" club; Negroes were admitted freely to the snack bar, poolroom, lounge and music room, but were "discouraged" from attending dances by being told there was another dance at "Club Number Two" with Negro girls available as partners. Negroes were not barred from *watching* dances at Club Number One, and whites often wandered into the largely Negro Club Number Two. The two noncoms said they served no liquor and had no trouble, handling race problems tactfully with no need for military police intervention.

Swimming pools, athletics, post canteens, movies on the base were all completely shared.

Lieutenant Colonel Harvey G. Johnson, "special services" or recreation officer, a Virginian, said that a chief worry at dances was whites trying to dance with Negro girls, or an occasional Negro back from combat in Korea who tried to dance with a white girl. He said such instances were broken up quickly because both whites and Negroes resented it.

"We tell them the Army has no regulations but we're bound to obey the customs of the community."

"This is a fine idea," Johnson said of the integration program. "The Army is getting more efficiency out of people. It even makes the whites better; they're afraid the colored will get the better of them."

Back in Columbia, G. A. Buchanan, Jr., editor of *The Record,* said there were no protests when Jackson was integrated, "significantly not even from the less educated group." He thought integration good militarily because "the Negro makes a better fighter in integrated units."

He concluded: "Segregation in the South must end gradually, yet gradualness is often the quickest way. I do not believe that anything that touches the deep-seated folkways of two peoples, as the abolition of segregation will, can wisely be done precipitately, so as to get beyond the support of public opinion."

FORT BRAGG, NORTH CAROLINA

Located in the North Carolina pine woods, Fort Bragg, one of the largest army bases in the nation, was the home of the famed All-American 82nd Airborne Division.

Sticks of parachutists — units of twelve men each — sat on the grass waiting to board planes for a test jump. A white sergeant in charge of one stick, whose men included a Negro noncom and two Negro privates, said the Negroes were okay.

Major General Charles D. W. Canham, commander of the 82nd, shouted above the roar of the planes, "It's working well; the Negro boys are extra sharp; they put the white boys on their mettle." He said Negroes in the unit showed no more fear of jumping than whites.

Major General Thomas F. Hickey, commandant of Fort Bragg, said that integration was "the only efficient way to use the manpower that's furnished us; if a Negro has the qualifications and a white man doesn't, it's a waste of manpower not to use the Negro." He added that many combat veterans thought integration was working "damn well," and "the consensus is that some of the Negroes are outstanding."

Colonel Broadus McAfee, Chief of Staff at Fort Bragg, said Negroes on the base held jobs in every military occupational specialty, in chemical, artillery, infantry, quartermaster and transportation units. Elementary schools, and family housing in some areas of the base, were unsegregated.

Robert L. Gray, city editor of the only newspaper in nearby Fayetteville, North Carolina, had served in Korea as an Air Force public information officer. He said he had been against racial mixing in the military but now favored it; it saved money and used skills of Negroes to the best advantage. He reported there was no stir among residents of Fayetteville, where segregation was still in full force, over the racial mixing at Bragg.

CAMP LEJEUNE, NORTH CAROLINA

A decade earlier the marines had no Negroes in their ranks. In 1942 Negroes were admitted to the Corps, but were strictly segregated as laborers, anti-aircraft gunners and ammunition handlers. By 1953 the color line had largely been erased at Lejeune, largest marine training base in the eastern United States.

"It's arrived," said Colonel Robert Luckey, Chief of Staff at Lejeune, base for the Second Marine Division. "They [Negroes] make good marines. Some have done heroic work in Korea. There's no trouble, no friction that I know of; it's become second nature, we don't bother about it any more."

Men were assigned to duty, he said, according to their military specialty — a rifleman to a rifle company, a radarman to a radar outfit. "The white boys work with the colored, sleep in the same barracks; Negro and white kids alike go to our schools, which are run under federal law." He related that in 1951, a Lejeune baseball team had been slated to play at the Tampa Bowl; Bowl authorities wouldn't admit a team including Negroes so the Lejeune team refused to play.

Luckey added that Negroes had their own club at Lejeune — "they like it."

A public information officer explained that dances held by

various units *as units* were non-segregated and men brought their own dates; official post dances, when hostesses were recruited by camp authorities, remained segregated because "white girls won't come with Negro girls."

Technical Sergeant James A. Watson of Brooklyn, New York, a Negro in charge of recreation for supply depot workers — white and Negro — was enthusiastic about the new Marine Corps. "There is no segregation anywhere in the marines," he said. "The old Uncle Tom Negro is gone, and we stand up and fight now; but if we do wrong, we expect to be punished just like the rest." He hoped to stay in service thirty years and put his sons through college. "There are a lot of things here I couldn't get on the outside," he explained.

A Negro desk sergeant in the base police station said there was never any race trouble he couldn't handle: "a little name calling, mostly by people of low intelligence."

The provost marshal, a white stockbroker from Ohio, rated the desk sergeant one of his best men. He said he himself had never seen any cases in which someone says, "That's a nigger, I'm going to hit him." "Beats the hell out of me," he added; "I'm glad it's here."

At the noncoms' club, white marines standing at the bar or dancing with their girls in the adjacent Mirror Room paid no attention when a Negro marine sergeant stepped up to the bar and ordered a bourbon. He talked about baseball to two white civilians standing near him. During a game of billiards later, a white marine waiter with a southern drawl asked the sergeant, "May I get you something, sir?"

The sergeant, a Philadelphian, told the author he was getting along fine in the marines. He said he had found no discrimination in barracks, work or elsewhere.

NORFOLK NAVY BASE, VIRGINIA

Through the Norfolk Navy Base at Norfolk, Virginia, passed some 8,000 sailors a week, coming and going from ships in port. In its schools men and women in navy blue learned radar, radio, teletyping, pipefitting, refrigeration, clerical work, even motion picture operation. The adjoining Naval Air Station trained men for carrier plane and patrol squadrons.

With certain exceptions the Norfolk base was racially integrated. Sailors attended the schools with no racial distinction in classes, barracks or mess halls.

But cafeterias, drinking fountains and rest rooms for civilian workers were still segregated,[1] and Negro and Filipino stewards who cared for officers' quarters ate and slept as separate units.

Rear Admiral Ralph O. Davis, commandant of the 5th Naval District covering the Norfolk Base, said the separate civilian facilities were essential because the workers came from Norfolk where segregation was the custom. He said the Negro stewards bunked and ate together because they worked together; if there were white stewards they would bunk with the Negroes.

He could recall no trouble of any kind with integration in the previous four years: "I think it has worked; I don't believe there are enough good Negroes that have come in to make any definite improvement in the overall Navy, but it has not been hurt since they put them all in together." Negroes at Norfolk, he added, "are on their mettle; they are getting better every year."

At the air conditioning and refrigeration school, five Negro sailors were working on intricate refrigeration equipment alongside white sailors. Lieutenant Frank L. Cherry from Oregon,

[1]That was at the time of the author's visit in the summer of 1952. The civilian facilities were being integrated in the fall of 1953 (see Chapter 23).

head of the school, said grades of the Negroes were "a little lower" than the white average but on the whole the Negroes were very good students and created no discipline problems: "They are here to learn."

Sylvester Hayes, 41-year-old Negro, said he joined the Navy as a mess attendant in 1933 but disliked what he felt to be the menial, segregated nature of the work. Returning to the Navy in World War II, he found it quite different; he had now transferred to the yeoman (office worker) school at Norfolk, and, "as far as I'm concerned, there's no discrimination whatsoever; everything is done now for the good of the Navy, not the white race."

A woman marine, Corporal Irma Locke, said she had wanted to go to college but when she tried to earn the money working at a soda fountain, she was fired because she was a Negro. A recruiting sergeant in Indianapolis, her home, "sort of let me know I could get ahead" in the Navy. A student at the yeoman school when interviewed, she described her life as "all ice cream and cake"; she figured girls must be more open-minded than men about race, but added that she often danced with white sailors at dances on the base.

At a PX cafeteria for uniformed personnel, groups of Negro and white sailors sat at tables together in conversation; other Negroes and whites were at tables to themselves. The same pattern — some mixed, some separate — was evident at open air beer gardens and seamen's clubs. At a post bowling alley, a Negro sailor was bowling with two white sailors.

At an enlisted men's club, several Negro sailors sat at tables alongside the crowded dance floor but none danced. A shore patrolman said Negro couples sometimes danced there but Negro sailors were not encouraged to dance with white girls: when such cases arose "we talk to the girl."

Off the base, Negroes encountered the sharp barrier of local segregation that surrounded nearly all southern military bases. Admiral Davis said he had tried to secure equal opportunities for recreation for Negro sailors off the base; "some of the best people in town have helped; we have a colored USO club now and are trying to improve it."

AIRCRAFT CARRIER FRANKLIN D. ROOSEVELT

Aboard the *FDR*, tied up at Norfolk, Negro and white sailors applied paint, loaded supplies and refitted the ship for its next cruise. One of the Navy's most modern flattops, this floating air base had a complement of about 2,500 officers and men (excluding its air group), about 100 of them Negroes. Some fifty to sixty of the Negroes served as stewards and the rest held "general service" ratings, working as engineers, gunners, signalmen, aircraft repairmen.

"There is no trouble," said Commander Turner F. Caldwell, the *FDR's* Executive Officer. "They are all mixed in, except that the stewards sleep separate since they are a separate bunch."

He considered racial integration an improvement over the former segregated system, removing a major source of tension and emotion — tension among Negroes and a sense of guilt among whites; the carrier had had no racial problems except one dockside brawl in which he said involvement of Negroes was incidental.

"It's the only policy that can work," he concluded. "The amount of work is so immense we can't afford additional problems of this kind."

Quartermaster First Class W. H. Richardson, a Negro, held the second-in-command post of the *FDR's* signaling unit. Described by his superior officers as outstanding, Richardson was in direct charge of the all-white, twenty-six signalman signal unit, and said he never had any difficulty as "boss" of white sailors. He got along so well with the southerners that "I only know the difference by their drawl."

Richardson said none of his many decisions, such as when to give leaves to his white crew, had ever been overruled by his superior officers.

"This is a new world I'm living in," he said. "There is no lack of opportunity to go up in the Navy according to your ability, though I don't think a Negro could become a captain or an admiral yet." In port at Norfolk, Richardson said he refused requests to go ashore with his white friends, "but I'm able to go with my buddies every place overseas."

Below the flight deck a Negro was directing a detail of white sailors checking in stores. Two Negroes practiced with the ship's band on a syncopated rhythm one of the Negroes had composed. Under the shade of a lifeboat, a white and a Negro sailor rested from paintbrush duty, elbows rubbing and talking amiably.

But in the stewards' sleeping quarters, Master-at-Arms James R. Stallworth, a husky Negro and top police officer over the Negro stewards, had this to say: "Our people don't like to pick up some officer's dirty clothes where he drops them, or pick up his pajamas from the floor. We don't want to be maids and butlers."

He said most Negroes hoped for the breakup of the Steward's Branch. Some were willing to give up their rank and start at the bottom to get out. "When the branch is gone, everything we do will be as a whole, not because we are one branch."

But once a steward, he added, it was hard to get transferred. "I worked as a barber for five years and tried to change my rate from steward to barber. I was told I couldn't and they gave me

no reason. One man here has 2,000 hours of commercial printing. He wanted to transfer to printing but was disapproved for
lack of men in the Steward's Branch. Submit the request ninety-
nine years from today and it will still be dismissed for lack of
stewards. I told my brothers not to come into the Navy as
stewards; I figure you can't get ahead in that branch."

Several Negro stewards who had gathered around to listen
nodded agreement. One said he had asked to transfer to other
duties but "they didn't even bother to tell me my transfer was
turned down."

Paul F. Baumann, a white lieutenant from San Marino, California, in charge of the *FDR* stewards, said he had had only one
application for a transfer from his stewards. He observed that
since stewards usually worked when other sailors were off duty,
this tended to segregate their social activities in addition to
their separate sleeping and eating facilities.

Ashore later, a white Virginian from the *FDR* crew said he
did not mind eating or sleeping with the two Negroes in his
section. But his companion, a Texan, said he always left the
table as quickly as possible when Negroes ate with him aboard
ship. He said he *knew* Negroes had a peculiar odor.

LOWRY AIR FORCE BASE, COLORADO

At Denver, Colorado, Brigadier General John T. Sprague,
base commander of Lowry Field, the Air Force Training
Command's chief photography school and one of its large gunnery training centers, discussed racial integration: "We have
them [Negroes] sprinkled all over the base, military and civilians. Our school for instructors is run by a Negro. This morning I was reviewing a crack gunnery drill team, led by a Negro
doing a crack job."

Asked how many Negroes were at Lowry, Sprague said he had no idea. "It's a sign of what's happening that I can't tell you," he said. "We don't think of them separately any more. Negroes were behind, but they're coming up. They depended on whites in the past, and have to learn to depend on themselves. They're about as good as whites in our courses here."

Was integration the best policy for the Air Force? "Oh yes," Sprague replied, "and that's a southerner speaking!"

The base public information officer, First Lieutenant Jack Taylor, said, "We sweated a bit" when a Negro and his wife moved into the officers' housing section, but there was no trouble of any kind. Southerners living nearby, he said, expressed amazement but no objection. He added that the Negro officer walked to classes with white officers, and their wives talked over the clothesline, but the families did not mix socially.

At a dance at the noncommissioned officers' club, three Negro couples sat at a front row table at the edge of the dance floor. From time to time a Negro couple got up and mingled with the white dancers. Two white airmen went over to the Negroes' table and sat down, talking and joking with the Negro airmen and their girls.

One of the club supervisors, a young wounded veteran of the Korean War, said that Negro couples "dance here all the time; there is no trouble of any kind; they are tactful; there is never any need for restraint."

General Sprague said Negroes from the base were accepted anywhere in Denver — at hotels, restaurants, shops.

"What worries me," said Sprague, "is that a military career for a Negro is now about the top he can get. It worries me whether we are going to have a predominantly Negro military service."

SEVENTEEN

The Deepest South

No more significant indicator of the social import of military non-segregation could be found than at Keesler Air Force Base, whose gates opened directly into the deep South city of Biloxi, Mississippi. Though Biloxi was a stronghold of segregation, Negro and white airmen had lived together on the adjoining base since 1949 with little or no ripple in day-to-day operations.

At a post rimmed by the Gulf of Mexico and brilliant with bougainvillaea and hibiscus, about 1,200 Negroes and 20,000 white airmen in May, 1953, studied radar, radio and control tower operation, or cooked the food, hauled the supplies and doctored the sick of the key Air Force electronics training center.

Major General James F. Powell, Virginia-born commander of Keesler, was admittedly skeptical about mixing Negroes and whites when the Air Force ordered integration in 1949. Now, four years later, he said there was "no more problem here than if the Negroes didn't exist."

He took the author on a tour of the base, pacing rapidly from classroom to classroom where Negroes and whites rubbed shoulders leaning over complicated radar equipment or watched instructors chalk diagrams of radio circuits on blackboards. In two classrooms, Negro civilians were teaching radar operation and fundamental electronics to white airmen.

Figures which Powell made available showed that the Negro washout rate was very slightly higher than the white rate. Grades of Negro airmen, according to base records, were "approximately the same average as all students."

At noon, Powell reviewed the change of classes as 9,000 airmen and Air Force women (Wafs) marched by in squadron formation. Negroes were in every squadron, scattered through the ranks, some holding the honor posts of colorbearer and line guide, a few wearing the green patch of class leader. A dozen or so Negro Wafs stepped smartly along in the Waf squadron, a tiny Negro Waf serving as line guide at the front of the column.

Later, in the barracks of one off-duty squadron, the men were listening to radios, sleeping, writing letters. An athletic young Negro in gym shorts and T-shirt was barracks leader of one dormitory, responsible for order among its white and Negro airmen; his superiors called him a good leader, and he reported complete satisfaction with his treatment and progress in the Air Force.

The major in charge of the squadron, a Georgian, demanded proof that the writer had been "cleared" to visit his squadron.

Satisfied, but asking that he not be quoted by name, he said he had been surprised but found the integration plan was "fine." Negroes and whites in his squadron borrowed each other's clothes with complete disregard of race.

He said that one evening he noticed three couples — three Negro airmen, two obviously Negro girls and one girl who looked like a "high yellow"—going into a canteen together.

"When I got close I found she was white," he said. "It's coming. I'm hardened to it. I'm from the South, but they're giving their blood the same as the white boys. There is no reason they shouldn't go around together if they want to."

Powell, the commander, had deliberately followed a go-slow policy on social aspects of integration, believing such an approach would cause less resentment among Biloxi townspeople. There was a strict, though informal, segregation of dances at nearly all base clubs. There was no racial label as such on clubs, but aside from the single lavish officers' club, distinctions were tacitly recognized. Thus everyone knew that the "Branch NCO Club" was intended for Negro noncoms. But lines were not strictly followed by the men and women themselves. At the Branch NCO Club, for example, a white airman had his arm in friendly fashion around two Negro airmen at the bar. A group of white airmen and their girl companions at one table were sandwiched between tables of Negro airmen with Negro girls.

Two white Wafs came in, ordered a pitcher of beer and sat quietly chatting at a table by themselves. One from New York and the other from Ohio, they said they resented some of the unofficial segregation practices they found at Keesler, such as the separate dances. One recounted indignantly how a Negro Waf had been stoned by a white girl walking on the sidewalk in Biloxi; but she added that the Negro Waf's roommate, a southern white girl, got along with her "just wonderfully."

There were other reports of discrimination of a secondary nature. A Negro sergeant, Joseph Jeffries of Vicksburg, Mississippi, said that barber shops at the base were segregated and Negroes were forced to wait hours for two Negro barbers while white airmen went to a base barber college and got quicker service. General Powell said this was because white barbers — local civilians — would not cut the hair of Negroes. He insisted that, in proportion to numbers, Negro airmen had a fair share of barbers.

A Negro psychiatrist on the base reported he had been able to rent a house in the officers' area only after lengthy protests to officials and letters to his congressman and senator. Though base officials denied this, the Negro officer's story dovetailed with Powell's avowed intent to go slow on "social" matters such as housing and dances.

Yet even those who reported instances of discrimination felt progress in racial relations at Keesler had been enormous. Jeffries related that a Negro boxing instructor at Keesler had been barred from the Biloxi USO where his base boxing team was to take part in a match. The instructor telephoned the base and Powell, refusing to permit discrimination, withdrew the team from the match.

A Negro chaplain said that, apart from dances and barber shops, there was no segregation on the base. "I'm just another chaplain," he said of his own duties; "fellows come to see me regardless of race." A native Mississippian, he said that Negro airmen now had an equal opportunity to get ahead, whereas in the past they had "unlimited opportunities to serve in foxholes only."

"It gives a fellow an answer to those who point to the ugly side, the enemies of democracy," he said. "It's like giving a man a stick to fight with, compared to a man without a stick. In the past he was defending something he didn't have — democracy. He has it now."

The Negro psychiatrist, despite his housing trouble, said that he had had almost no friction with other white doctors, or with patients — many of them from the South. Taking his turn as Officer of the Day to handle medical complaints after duty hours, he said that some patients "gulped when they saw me, but none said they didn't want me to treat them — women, children, men." One white medic told him an officer's wife "made unkind remarks about me"; the hospital commandant, informed by the medic, forbade her to enter the hospital again.

The psychiatrist, a native of Long Island, New York, said he had successfully treated several difficult mental cases involving wives of white officers and men, and they had gratefully sent him letters of thanks and Christmas cards. Housed between white officers, he said his immediate neighbors accepted him and his wife and that they frequently played bridge at a white neighbor's home.

"The encouraging thing about it," he added, "is that so many of the younger people are free of prejudice; they've accepted integration without a struggle."

As significant as the non-segregation at Keesler was its impact on the people of Biloxi, where not many years since a Negro would automatically have stepped into the street to let a white person pass.

Powell said there was no question that community feelings had changed since integration began at Keesler. He said that in the early days he had stopped holding parades in town due to complaints about Negroes marching with whites; now there was no objection at all and he called attention to the fact that Negro and white airmen were to take part in parades and entertainment at Biloxi's nearing, annual shrimp festival.

He said he had refused for a time to send the base's racially mixed choir to sing at distant charity or other entertainments because local custom barred the Negro and white singers from eating or sleeping together on overnight trips and he refused to let them be segregated. But he said members of the choir had been served lunch together recently at one of the smart hotels on the nearby resort coast—"probably the first time any colored boy ate at any hotel in Mississippi."

Negro airmen also reported a changed attitude in town. Not long previously, a Negro entering a Biloxi store would have waited until all white customers were served. The Negro psychiatrist at Keesler, a captain in rank, said he was always treated courteously in downtown shops, with white salesgirls asking politely, "May I help you, sir?"

There was still a strict ban on serving Negroes in local restaurants or cafes. On one occasion base officials suffered acute embarrassment when a dark-skinned, but non-Negro, foreign military student training at Keesler ran into this color bar without advance warning.

Taxidrivers hauling airmen from base to town ran into an odd dilemma. Local law forbade them to haul Negroes and whites in the same taxi; but Powell would not let them discriminate on the base. The drivers worked out a compromise. They hauled Negroes and whites together while on the base, without charge, to a taxi stand at the gate; then either Negroes or whites would get out and take another cab downtown.

One cab driver explained that residents of Biloxi did not care what happened on the base, but "they can't do it in town — they'd arrest them."

"They'll be eating and sleeping together in the rest of the country one of these days," he declared. "I hear they do it already in some places."

Negro airmen seeking entertainment in Biloxi could find it only in the Negro section of town, with little to offer but low-grade "dives" and illicit gambling dens. Powell and other base officials had long sought to obtain a Negro USO in town, since Negroes were barred from the white USO club. Funds for a Negro USO were finally included in a bond issue which became a target of political rivalry in the 1953 Biloxi mayoralty election.

The Biloxi chief of police, Earl Wetzel, told the author that a white man found in the Negro section of town was arrested as a matter of course. A soft-spoken, bespectacled man, he discussed readily the difference in beliefs of people in Biloxi from those in many northern areas.

"I don't believe we're mistreating our niggers," he said. "We keep to ourselves socially, and they live in their part of town; but we work together with them. We have the best niggers in the South in this town."

Regarding non-segregation at Keesler Field, he remarked that the Constitution said people are equal and guessed the government had to live up to it.

Asked if there had been objections to integration when it was begun at Keesler, he said there had been no "official complaints, only rumors; when we'd trace them down, we'd find some damn ignoramus; now nobody says anything about it."

"Negroes are being treated better everywhere," he continued. "Maybe in two-three generations you won't know white from colored. It's what people are taught as children that makes them what they are."

Major John P. Wolcott, Troop Executive in charge of thirty-five squadrons at Keesler Field and a native of Biloxi, stated that he believed all Americans would accept nonsegregation more and more as time went on; men leaving the service, he said, would retain at least some of their experience.

"In time, perhaps not in my lifetime, Negroes will have equal status — though perhaps not socially," he said. "Our airmen who are discharged have different views in civilian life than they had before. It happens more and more every day. They are learning to live with Negroes."

EIGHTEEN
Working Like Yeast

In February, 1953, Colonel James F. Olive, Jr., commander of Harlingen Air Force Base, Texas, received the following letter:

"Dear Colonel Olive: It is with pleasure that we inform you of the following motion that was unanimously passed by the session of our church Wednesday, February 11, 1953: 'That the commanding officer of the Harlingen Air Force Base be asked to invite all officers and airmen of the . . . Base, regardless of race or color, to attend any or all of our church services.' This action came about as a result of our observance last week of Race Relations Sunday. We will appreciate any action you may take that will make the officers and airmen under your command, regardless of race or color, feel free to worship God with us in our church. We commend the actions of the Air Force in your pro-

149

gram of eliminating race discrimination, and hope that our action may be at least a step forward in uniting our people as one under God."

The letter was dated February 12, Lincoln's Birthday. It was signed by H. Richard Copeland, Minister, and D. A. Crossley, Clerk of the Session, First Presbyterian Church, Brownsville, Texas.

Two generations ago Brownsville had been the scene of one of the most notorious Negro troop riots in United States history. Prior to Copeland's letter, probably no Negro had ever been admitted to a white Protestant church in Brownsville. Colonel Olive, replying, called the action "a movement of far-reaching importance, and one which displays moral courage and an open willingness to abide by your Christian convictions."

Racial integration in the military was exercising a powerful influence on civilian habits; it was inevitable that it should.

Expressing this point of view, Mrs. Anna Rosenberg, Assistant Secretary of Defense until January 1, 1953, told this writer, "In the long run, I don't think a man can live and fight next to one of another race, and share experiences where life is at stake, and not have a strong feeling of understanding when he comes home."

Major General Charles I. Carpenter, chief of Air Force chaplains, put it this way: "You can't turn a million guys into the military this year, and have them live and work together without segregation, without some impression when they return to their own communities. Integration is already having an impact, though not out in the open. It is working like yeast, quietly."

Reports began spreading of case after case in which tight civilian racial restrictions were relaxed in favor of Negro servicemen. Air Force files told how, in Amarillo, Texas, long a bulwark of segregation, the USO club was opened to Negro and white airmen alike; and officials at the Amarillo Air Base persuaded Amarillo University to admit Negroes along with white airmen to its extension classes.

At Larson Air Force Base, a program of co-operation with the nearby town of Moses Lake, Washington, led a local couple to offer a home dinner as a door prize at a dance. A Negro airman won and the couple invited him and a Negro buddy to dinner. Their host discovered they were fishing enthusiasts and took them on a week-end fishing trip.

In many areas, North and West as well as South, Negro servicemen were still barred from most facilities — particularly of a social nature — in towns near military posts. In many such communities, the only places Negroes could go for entertainment were breeding grounds for venereal disease, vice and resulting lowered military performance.

All military services had striven to secure more off-base facilities for Negro as well as white servicemen. The commander of the Rapid City, South Dakota, Air Force Base asked leading property owners in Rapid City, which had few Negro dwellers, to lease one unit of property apiece to Negro couples, whom he promised to select carefully. By mid-summer of 1952 he had placed five Negro airmen's families, with no reported repercussions. By then Negro airmen could eat at three of Rapid City's best restaurants, previously barred to them.

But in Yuma, Arizona, the townspeople were reportedly so unhospitable to Negroes at one period that a dispatch to Washington in 1952 said all Negro airmen were being transferred out of the nearby air base.

A study of relationships between Negroes at integrated U.S. Army posts and civilians in nearby towns was conducted by a team of social scientists, as part of the comprehensive survey of army integration discussed in Chapter 13. They interviewed 1,508 military personnel and 771 civilians — from clerks and secretaries to social workers, store owners, bartenders, cab drivers, policemen, waitresses and ministers — at five bases in both North and South.

Using what is called a "critical incident" technique, the researchers reported on 824 incidents involving off-post relations between Negro GI's and white civilians. Significantly, the vast bulk of incidents reported as "favorable" by *both Negroes and whites, including civilians,* involved instances in which Negroes were treated *without discrimination.*

The social scientists, this author and others found a few cases in which white prejudice against Negroes had deepened, or developed where there had been none before, due to contact with Negroes in integrated military units. But these were a small minority compared to the overwhelming number of instances in which whites acquired new understanding, even personal friendship, toward Negroes they met in service.

In the field of employment, military racial integration had done much to open the door of opportunity to Negroes.

George L. P. Weaver, director of the CIO Civil Rights Committee, told this writer that elimination of segregation in the military made it much easier to secure jobs with government contractors for competent Negroes. In days of military segregation, he said, these employers cited official segregation as evidence that the government did not intend to enforce the nondiscrimination clause in federal contracts. "But now that argument is gone."

Men who received training in military skills were getting ahead for the first time on the basis of qualifications, not race, Weaver said. "There have been countless instances where training in the armed forces can be used as an acceptable criterion of fitness and ability." Negroes were using their military skills to get good jobs in many industries, he said — aircraft production, auto, telephone, radio and electronics among the most prominent. He felt industrial opportunities for Negroes would increase as military integration continued.

Weaver said the military pattern also helped CIO representatives obtain entrance for Negroes to vocational schools and apprenticeships. "We can point to boys who have been trained in the military to show it will work," he said. He added that private vocational schools, which often guaranteed jobs to their graduates, had turned down Negro trainees in the past for lack of job opportunities upon graduation; "now we can point to companies that will hire trained Negroes, and training schools are enrolling more and more Negro boys."

Dwight R. G. Palmer, Board Chairman of General Cable Corporation of New York and a member of the Fahy Committee, said: "Along with the uniform goes a halo of bravery and good Americanism. If the uniformed man practices outside what he learns inside the camp, the missionary circuit is completed and his civilian associates follow his lead."

NINETEEN

Democracy's New Salesmen

"In America, I saw lynch law once more. In Portland, for example, a Negro once happened to enter a beer parlor. This was enough to have a group of young Americans throw him to the ground in the street and beat him fiercely with anything they could lay their hands on, about the head, face, and stomach. All this took place in daylight in a downtown street in front of a crowd that had gathered. No one could intervene because Truman, the boss of Wall Street, encouraged racial discrimination . . ."

That was an excerpt from a Soviet broadcast in November, 1949. Communist propaganda after World War II capitalized heavily on treatment of Negro minorities in the United States. Seizing on every instance of brutality or discrimination as fresh evidence of a "master race" complex, Kremlin propagandists sought to convince the world — particularly its darker peoples — that the United States was the enemy of anyone not born with a white skin.

"The race theory is one of the clearest signs of the fascistization of contemporary America," wrote I. Lapitsky in the Soviet magazine *Trud* in May, 1951. "The violent manifestation of reaction within the country is directly linked with the aggressive foreign policy plans of the American imperialists and with their mad idea to establish a world hegemony."

Russia's race propaganda, a skillful blend of half-truths and lies, had done the United States untold damage in the eyes of millions throughout the world. During 1952, State Department officials reported that U.S. overseas libraries received more requests for material on American racial problems than any other continuing subject matter.

Secretary of State Dean Acheson, in a statement to the Supreme Court December 2, 1952, in connection with hearings on public school segregation, said that during the preceding six years the damage to United States foreign relations attributable to racial resentment abroad had become "progressively greater." . . . "The continuance of racial discrimination in the United States remains a source of constant embarrassment to this government in the day-to-day conduct of its foreign relations; and it jeopardizes the effective maintenance of our moral leadership of the free and democratic nations of the world."

State Department specialists on foreign opinion catalogued for this writer some of the areas where Russia's racial propaganda had hurt America most. In Latin America, particularly Argentina, Communist and nationalist propaganda had combined to attack discrimination in this country, sometimes becoming "viciously anti-U.S." In India, Africa and Southeast

Asia, anti-American sentiment was inflamed by reports of suppression of Negroes in the United States, skillfully tied in by Communist propagandists with colonial desires for independence.

The Indian weekly *Blitz*, a sensational, pro-Communist newspaper with wide reader appeal in Bombay, contained an article in its February 9, 1952, issue entitled "We Charge Genocide," which echoed a more recent Russian propaganda theme that the United States was trying literally to exterminate darker races. Referring to the Ku Klux Klan as a "gangster-gunman" organization whose "savagery against the Negro people is perhaps the most organized effort to terrorize the Negro," *Blitz* asserted, "Few know that this gangster organization has the official support of the government," in fact is "hired by the government as its strong-arm to silence the Negro people."

The West had received many warnings that it could not ignore such attacks, as it might have done in the days when opinion throughout the eastern half of the globe was controlled by western nations. A Negro labor expert with the U.S. Point Four program in Burma wrote to a friend in the Pentagon in 1953: "It cannot be overemphasized that the policies and implementation of policies affecting countries in this part of the world are no longer made in the capitals of London, Paris and Washington by white people but are now made in Rangoon, New Delhi, Djakarta and Saigon by dark people."

Even among America's closest allies, the racial issue had cast suspicion on the United States as a champion of freedom and equality.

Some western nations, it is true, practiced their own forms of race discrimination, particularly among their colonial peoples; for a time U.S. Negro troops were barred from a dozen or more areas, chiefly British colonies, though by 1953 such prohibitions were mostly gone except for Iceland, where State Department officials said Negroes were not wanted.

But in the eyes of friendly nations as with most others, this country's segregation system had chiefly been seen as a highly vulnerable target in the ideological cold war with Communism. That, said government officials, was why developments like the ending of military segregation could play such a prominent role in the worldwide battle for men's minds. The problem was to get the story across.

The U.S. Information Service had sent films, pamphlets, lecturers to all parts of the world, spreading news of nonsegregation developments. Integration of the military was a growing theme in this story. Fifty thousand copies of a report on minorities in America, including information on military non-segregation, were distributed in Vienna, in 1952.

American movies showing racial equality were prized by United States propagandists for their probable effect abroad. Officials of the Eisenhower administration quietly suggested to Hollywood producers that a forthcoming film featuring the U.S. Military Academy at West Point include casual shots of Negro cadets at the Academy.

Even more telling could be the influence of American servicemen all over the world. An official report received at the State Department told of the "marked contribution" to U.S.-Pakistan relations rendered by the visit of a naval cruiser division to Karachi in August, 1948. With "skillful public relations" that led to friendly press coverage, several misconceptions about the United States were removed, notably those relating to racial problems, the report stated. It cited a columnist in the Karachi *Daily Gazette,* who wrote, "What struck me most was the complete absence of any color bar on board the ship. There were Negro sailors, Filipinos and whites, and they seemed to be on good terms with one another and also with their officers."

U.S. psychological warfare experts cited the lack of racial propaganda by Communist forces during the Korean War as evidence that integration of U.S. troops had dulled the edge of the Russian propaganda weapon in that area. One of the Negro prisoners released by the Communists in the sick and wounded prisoner exchange in early 1953 just laughed when asked if Communist propaganda had had any effect on him. The Communists, in fact, went to the trouble of separating Negro and white American prisoners in some Korean prison camps to halt the "buddying" which contradicted the Soviet propaganda claim.

Sergeant Edward Hewlett of Detroit, a returned Negro war prisoner, told newspapermen that the Communists tried repeatedly to get him to write articles "exposing" racial discrimination in the United States. He was quoted as saying that other Negroes were similarly approached but "not very many men did."

An English visitor to America told this writer that he had overheard British girls in London commenting on Negro and white U.S. soldiers walking together, saying that Americans were really practicing democracy in their armed forces.

It was too early in 1953 to tell just how effective the observable fact of racial integration of the U.S. military would be in weakening the traditional foreign view of this country as a "master race" nation where Negroes were concerned. Communist propaganda had striven mightily to belittle the United States military integration program.

Officials of the Eisenhower administration, wrestling with the problem of America's world status, were acutely aware of the part race would continue to play in the psychological battle against Communism. Members of the special committee under

William H. Jackson, named by President Eisenhower to study the best way to conduct American anti-Communist propaganda, concluded that this country should concentrate more of its time and money on winning the friendship of peoples of Africa, Asia and the Middle East, who were torn between Communism and democracy, than on already friendly nations. The men planning to follow up this change of emphasis felt that this country's official non-segregation policies — freshly strengthened by Eisenhower's strong anti-segregation pronouncements — should be given a major role in efforts to convince peoples of these so-called "third areas" that the United States was their friend and ally.

"It puts us on their side in their drive for national identity," one administration official explained.

Japan in 1953 was one of the critical areas where U.S. practices and propaganda would play a crucial part in determining the ultimate gravitation of the people to the East or West. The following incident was told to the author in May, 1953, by a captain stationed at U.S. Army headquarters in Tokyo, during a brief visit to this country.

A Japanese college student, attending a discussion meeting at a center maintained by the Quakers in Tokyo, was most inquisitive about America's handling of racial problems. Quoting from a book in his hand, he asked Americans present if there still were nine million slaves in the United States. The captain, who was present, tried to explain the racial situation in the United States. He described the military integration program, and noted that white and Negro American officers lived together in Tokyo; he said he had two Negro officers sharing his room. The student appeared unconvinced. The captain asked to see the source of his figures. "Sure enough, it was good old Lenin," he observed.

After the session the Japanese student was invited to join the Americans for ice cream and coffee at the Yuraku Hotel, a center for American officers. Quite by chance, said the captain, Negro and white officers were sitting together at several tables when they reached the hotel.

The Japanese student said nothing but "you could see him taking it in." The captain added that prior to this time the student had been leaning toward Communism, and subsequently he became a strong advocate of democracy and went to work on a leading Japanese newspaper.

Mrs. Anna Rosenberg, Assistant Secretary of Defense in charge of manpower in 1952, summed up the feeling of many government leaders when she said the importance of military integration in the international picture "can't be overestimated; it's a living example of democracy in action — the only answer to Communist propaganda."

TWENTY

The Woman Problem

A special board, set up by Navy Secretary Frank Knox in 1941 to investigate complaints about the Navy's racial policy, recommended against using Negroes outside the Messman's Branch. In doing so, it said this limitation was only a part of the American pattern of discrimination which in turn was due partly to the fact that the white man "refuses to admit the Negro to intimate family relationships leading to marriage."

"These concepts are not truly democratic, but it is doubtful if the most ardent lovers of democracy will dispute them, particularly in regards to intermarriage," the board said.

Fear of racial intermarriage had been stressed for years as the chief argument against non-segregation in America. Dwight R. G. Palmer, industrialist member of the Fahy Committee, said that military officials who appeared before the committee to oppose integration "always rang in a bedroom scene."

Abraham Lincoln, debating the slavery issue in 1857, protested against "that counterfeit logic which concludes that, because I do not want a black woman for a slave I must necessarily want her for a wife. . . . In some respects she certainly is not my equal; but in her natural right to eat the bread she earns with her own hands without asking leave of anyone else, she is my equal, and the equal of all others."[1]

Whatever the reasoning, the "woman problem" had usually been considered the "thin ice" edge of the military integration program.

Gunnar Myrdal, the Swedish sociologist, in his book, *An American Dilemma,* cited a study showing that whites resisted mingling with Negroes most strongly when it came to sex and marriage; after that in social contacts; and on down a descending scale of opposition, with jobs and housing at the bottom. Ten years later army researchers, in opinion surveys in Korea and the United States, found much the same attitude: white GI's were most interested in keeping Negroes apart when it came to personal contacts involving white women. In interviews with soldiers on U.S. bases and civilians in nearby communities, no whites reported favorably any contacts between Negroes and white women; thirty-six cited as "unfavorable" incidents in which Negro soldiers approached or tried to date civilian white women.

When it came to on-post social relations, racially mixed dancing was least favored by white soldiers. But, surprising many military men, objections were not strong enough to cause trouble. Of 2,351 white GI's, questioned as to what they thought

[1] *Abraham Lincoln, His Speeches and Writings,* edited by Roy P. Basler.

an imaginary "Joe Doakes" would do if he saw a Negro couple at a post dance, 73 percent said Joe would pay no special attention; others thought Joe would ask the Negro to leave, or walk out himself; only one percent predicted he would try to get friends to beat up the Negro.

On an even touchier question, a Negro dancing with a white girl, 33 percent said Private Doakes would pay no attention and 27 percent said he would watch to see if the girl wanted someone to cut in — in other words, a majority predicted more or less passive acceptance so long as the white girl was not distressed; others said Joe would leave, complain to authorities or cut in without waiting; only 5 percent predicted he would try to persuade friends to beat up the Negro.

"Joe" was assumed to mirror attitudes of the men questioned. The researchers reported that actual developments backed up the predictions. Where Negro couples danced among white couples only minor friction occurred. Even in the few reported instances of racially mixed couples, predictions of trouble failed to materialize.

Studies and surveys revealed a pattern in dances on military posts. In the North, they were generally attended by Negro couples as well as whites. Negroes occasionally danced with white girls, and white men with Negro girls. In some communities in the North and far West, white girls invited as hostesses to air bases were advised in advance it would be proper for them to dance with Negro airmen if asked.

James Madison, Negro field representative of the National Recreation Association and unpaid consultant to the Air Force, said such orientation was given white hostesses by USO officials at such places as Philadelphia, San Francisco and Yakima, Washington, where girls were recruited to attend dances at nearby air bases.

In San Francisco, he elaborated, hostesses were given to understand they were to entertain all service personnel regardless of race or nationality. "They are given an 'out,'" he added. "If they refuse to dance with a man for any reason other than improper conduct, they must refuse all other partners for the rest of that number." The hostesses, of course, served on a purely voluntary basis.

Madison reported that at one New England air base, when girls from neighboring communities refused to dance with Negro airmen, the GI advisory committee composed of enlisted men on the base decided unanimously it wanted no girls who refused to dance with all airmen. New hostesses were soon recruited who did not reject Negro partners, Madison added.

In the South, dancing presented a more difficult problem. Nearly all communities were accustomed to strict social segregation, and girls with such backgrounds might refuse to attend dances at all if Negroes were present. There was also apprehension of trouble from local communities if Negroes tried to dance with southern white girls. Therefore interracial dancing — a white with a Negro partner — was quietly discouraged, or banned outright, in most southern posts of all services. Separate dances were usually held for Negroes, though an occasional Negro couple appeared at white dances and a larger number of whites attended Negro dances; isolated instances of interracial dancing were reported.

Another area where Negroes might come in contact with white women was at swimming pools, to which guests could usually be invited.

"Now I've seen everything!" commented a general on one southern base as he passed the post pool and counted about forty white girls amidst a large number of Negro and white soldiers.

The Army's researchers found varying practices in the use of swimming pools. One officer reported that Negro and white men were allowed to use a base pool freely but no dependents were admitted, thus eliminating the possibility of contacts between men and women of different races. Pools were shared by Negro and white men, however, with no friction in both the North and South.

Despite widely differing practices in these and other off-duty activities, it was apparent that military racial integration was increasing the contacts of Negroes and whites of opposite sexes. Whether this was likely to lead to increasing racial intermarriage was conjectural at this stage. Major General Charles I. Carpenter, chief of Air Force chaplains, said that to the best of his knowledge the only racial intermarriages in the Air Force were occurring in foreign countries, chiefly Germany and Japan, where there was less social objection to Negroes than in the United States, and where mixed military marriages had not been uncommon when Negroes were still segregated.

Some military officials feared many interracial GI marriages taking place abroad would break up when the couples returned to this country and the girls learned the full extent of their social problems. One high-ranking officer, strongly in favor of the integration program, was worried that mixed marriages among American Negro GI's abroad might be "the most dangerous thing that can happen to the whole [integration] program."

Military authorities also faced a problem of where to assign racially mixed GI couples returning to this country. Most southern states not only barred racial intermarriage but prohibited interracial cohabitation outright. It was the policy of all services not to assign a mixed couple to such states, and authorities at the Pentagon tried to keep watch over such cases.

But sometimes a mistake occurred. One Negro serviceman

with a white wife was assigned to a southern army post by error. State authorities could not interfere as long as the couple remained on the post; when they secured housing in town, both were promptly clapped in jail, and freed only when the Negro secured a transfer to a northern base.

Two other aspects of the "woman problem" bore on the military's racial program. The venereal disease rate among Negro troops as a whole had always been higher than for white soldiers, though a few Negro units with good leadership and high morale occasionally wiped out almost all traces of social disease. Figures available in the Army Surgeon General's office showed that overall Negro VD rates in the Army were about 6.8 times the white rate in 1918, 5.7 times in 1945 and about 5 times the white rate in 1952.

Army medical authorities said in 1953 that, while they had no significant statistics yet on the impact of integration on the VD rate, there was good reason to believe the Negro rate would drop steadily under conditions of non-segregation and tend to approach the white norm in time.

They said that in general the higher rate among Negroes could be traced to poorer economic and educational backgrounds, a less inhibited approach to sex, and restricted opportunities for association with "acceptable" women. In integrated living conditions, these officials felt Negroes would be more likely to adopt the standards of the white majority, exercise greater care in personal hygiene and use of prophylactics, and spend more time in recreation on the base, or in town with white comrades in higher level entertainment than normally available to Negroes alone.

It has been noted that Assistant Army Secretary Fred Korth did in fact find a steady decline in the overall Army VD rate in Europe after integration took place.

Many military officials also believed that crimes of violence, including rape, would tend to decrease among Negro troops under integrated service. Military court-martial records contradicted exaggerated reports of wholesale Negro rapes in Europe at the close of World War II. From July 18, 1942, to November 1, 1946, 205 white and 256 Negro soldiers were convicted of rape by general courts-martial in the European theater, and authorities said there were only one or two Negro rape convictions in the China-Burma-India theater compared to five or six whites.

No comparable records were available for the Korean War, due in part to the fact that the Army Judge Advocate General's office had dropped racial labels from its crime records several years earlier. However, JAG officials said that legal advisers of army divisions in Korea agreed unanimously that Negro military offenses decreased after integration took place.

The higher Negro "incident" rate boosted the rate of white units in Europe when integration began there, but then the combined rate began a steady decline, these officials added.

The Judge Advocate General's office did not believe rapist "tendencies" of individuals would be affected immediately by military integration. But JAG officials, who acknowledged that Negro rape and other crime rates had always been higher than white rates in the Army, believed integration might reduce the temptation toward Negro rapes by cutting the likelihood of Negro "ganging," and inducing Negroes to spend more off-duty time on the post.

Two final incidents, while not justifying conclusions on the "woman problem" aspect of military non-segregation, may at least provide clues for future researchers.

Jet magazine for June 25, 1953, reported that a white Air Force sergeant from Wisconsin became acquainted with a Negro civilian woman employee while both were at the Lake Charles, Louisiana, Air Force Base. He met secretly with the girl, a native of Lake Charles, proposed marriage and was told in reply he was "crazy" to suggest such a thing in Louisiana, where the law forbade interracial marriage.

Jet, a Negro publication, said that after his discharge the sergeant persuaded the girl, with the help of an Air Force friend at the Lake Charles Base, to go to Minneapolis where they were married by a Negro minister. The pair were quoted after the ceremony as saying, "There's nothing unusual about it. We met, fell in love and married. We will be glad, though, when the laws of the South change so we can go back" to visit the bride's parents.

A southern politician, in a speech to students at a large southern military school, was reported to have emphasized his pro-segregation views by asking, "You wouldn't want your sister to marry a Negro, would you?"

According to the story, the students promptly began to chant as if by prearrangement: "She can say no, can't she? She can say no, can't she?"

TWENTY-ONE
Into the Classroom

A by-product of military racial integration, which likewise could have a deep impact on civilian patterns in the United States, was the movement to end segregated schooling for children of service personnel.

With the same lack of publicity that marked racial integration in the military services, the system of segregated schools on some military bases began to vanish. By the summer of 1953, federally operated schools had quietly opened their doors to children of all races living on at least eight southern army, navy, Air Force and marine bases. The last existing segregated federal school, at Fort Benning, Georgia, began operating on a non-segregated basis with the 1953 fall term. Steps were under way, with the personal backing of President Eisenhower, to end segregation in some twenty-one schools operated by state or local agencies on southern bases.

The story of integration in each southern base school was a drama in itself. Take the case of Fort Bragg, North Carolina.

Mrs. Mildred Poole, a white North Carolinian by birth, was trained in teaching in her native state, and also in New York and Tennessee. She came to Fort Bragg as principal of its elementary school in the fall of 1947.

Following the law of the state, only children of white soldiers then attended the school. Children of Negro soldiers were taken by bus to segregated schools in nearby communities.

Mrs. Poole was oppressed by growing complaints from Negro parents, who protested that their children did not get an "equal" education or even a "good" education in the local Negro schools.

She had no ready answer. She saw the Army start to integrate the children's fathers, but she had no word on what to do about the children. After the Korean War began, she was confronted with a congressional directive to operate the post schooling as cheaply as possible.

The troubled principal decided to force a decision. Preparing her budget for the 1951-52 school year, Mrs. Poole stated that the money would be used for a non-segregated school. The Fort Bragg school board and the base commander, Lieutenant General John W. Leonard, approved the plan — a "daring and noble thing for them to do," Mrs. Poole said later. The budget was forwarded to the U.S. Office of Education in Washington, which handled funds appropriated by Congress for military schools.

The budget came back, approved without comment. Mrs. Poole opened her school on an integrated basis for the first time in September, 1951. It was almost a month later before her action received outside attention, when an Associated Press dispatch reported the innovation.

"Mail, mail, mail" said Mrs. Poole later. Many letters praised the principal; some upbraided her, accusing her of undermining the southern way of life. Three threatened her life.

"They never worried me," she said, "because I knew it was right."

But no word came from army headquarters in Washington or from the Office of Education.

Early in 1952, Mrs. Poole went to Washington and talked to W. B. Coleman, Office of Education official who had handled the Fort Bragg budget. She related that he demanded to know by what authority she had opened a non-segregated school.

Amazed, Mrs. Poole replied that she did so only after he and the Education Office approved her budget calling for one.

"They were dumbfounded," she recalled. The Office of Education had apparently not noticed the word "non-segregated" in her budget, and her program had been approved by mistake.

Meanwhile at Fort Bragg, the integrated school had gone into operation smoothly and with almost no difficulty. Mrs. Poole said she had only one complaint when it was announced the school would end segregation, from an officer's wife who "tearfully phoned me and said her husband had forbidden her to send their daughter to school with Negroes; he was going to send her back home with the child."

The children themselves had little trouble. Friendships sprang up almost immediately between the white and Negro youngsters.

Mrs. Poole told of one Negro girl in the sixth grade who was stung in the face by a wasp. A general's daughter brought her to the principal, then asked permission to go with her in a bus to the dispensary. "I think she's scared," explained the little girl.

Colonel Tyler Calhoun, Jr., of Nashville, Tennessee, base chief of staff at the time, had two children of his own in the post school. He told of his five and one-half-year-old daughter's first day in kindergarten. "I asked her if there was any colored child in her class. 'Yes,' she replied. 'His name is Butch and he can wiggle his ears. He's going to teach us how to wiggle ours.'"

One Negro mother, wife of a master sergeant, said her six-year-old daughter had no trouble whatsoever, except that "a couple of times they called her 'black' and she heard the word 'nigger' for the first time."

The mother said the white parents are the ones who should "really get a little education."

A Negro paratroop sergeant's wife, mother of children aged twelve, fourteen and fifteen, said, "It's just wonderful; it's the first experience they ever had in a mixed school and it's helped us a great deal." Asked if her children had run into any difficulties, she said, "None whatsoever."

Although there was general acceptance of the unsegregated school, a few white parents remained dubious. The wife of a post plumber said, "I was born and raised in the South and it's been kind of hard for me, but the children settle their own differences."

Mrs. Poole said her staff had been "very co-operative." There was some grumbling at first about bringing in Negro children, but she said some of the grumblers complained later because they didn't get Negroes in their classes. School enrollment totaled about 1,500 in the 1951-52 and 1952-53 years, with Negro children usually numbering between thirty and fifty.

There was one Negro teacher on the staff of sixty the first year, but her husband was transferred and she did not return for the 1952-53 year. The principal hoped to get a proportionate number of Negro teachers "because you can discriminate there too."

Mrs. Poole said the school "never had the first problem between a teacher and a child, a child and a child, or a parent and a parent; all the difficulty came from outside."

For example, she entered her school in a dancing and singing contest with outside schools only to realize that one of her talented Negro boys was "sure to win" the post school's dancing contest, and would represent the school in the outside competition. This could have caused much embarrassment; outside white schools might have refused to compete if a Negro was a contestant. The parents suggested their son be eliminated, but Mrs. Poole said that would be discrimination. She offered to turn down the base school's invitation to participate. The boy finally agreed to compete only in the singing contest; he was eliminated in the post trials; and possible embarrassment was avoided.

Mrs. Poole concluded: "It's a Christian problem and it's been kind of fun. It's history and it's been one of the greatest challenges of my life."

At the Pentagon in Washington, Mrs. Poole's "test case" was being closely watched along with other such experiments, although she did not know it. Officials concerned with military racial policies officially ignored integration of southern base schools.

"Our strategy at the time was to leave them alone," one official explained. "We wanted to let two or three of these non-segregated schools spring up spontaneously rather than initiate a formal policy" which might have invited southern congressmen to object and perhaps block further progress.

President Truman, however, evidently was kept informed. On November 2, 1951, he vetoed a bill, one provision of which he said would have forced schools on military posts "now operating successfully on an integrated basis to be segregated" in states requiring segregated schools.

At this time both federally and locally run schools for children on northern and western military posts were unsegregated, according to prevailing state patterns; but locally run schools were segregated on all southern bases.

Months passed and little was done about post schools in the South. The integrated schools continued without trouble. On May 1, 1952, a white Minnesota mother, wife of a serviceman stationed at Fort Bliss, Texas, wrote a letter to her senator, Hubert H. Humphrey of Minnesota.

She protested that Jim Crow laws in Texas, under which white children attended school on the post and Negroes went to segregated schools in nearby El Paso, were a "violation of the civil rights of my child."

The letter was one of hundreds of thousands pouring into Congress every year. It would normally be routine to answer it. But Humphrey also sent it to Assistant Secretary of Defense Anna M. Rosenberg with a request for a report.

The letter caused no immediate stir, but a year later, looking back, officials saw it as the trigger that touched off formal steps to integrate the entire system of military dependent schools. A copy of the letter, now in a Pentagon file, bears the notation, "This letter started the whole inquiry."

Mrs. Rosenberg, replying to Humphrey on June 16, cited a clause in the law under which the Fort Bliss school operated. She said it barred any federal control over the post school. Humphrey relayed the reply to Mrs. Ferry, saying, "I regret this situation very much but since this is statutory, our hands are tied."

Strangely, President Truman's veto message of November 2,

1951, with its implied support for non-segregated schools, had been overlooked by Mrs. Rosenberg's office and by Humphrey.

Five months after Mrs. Ferry wrote to Humphrey, on October 2, 1952, Clarence Mitchell, Washington representative of the National Association for the Advancement of Colored People, brought the veto back into the picture. He wrote to Defense Secretary Robert A. Lovett calling segregation in post schools a "shocking departure" from Mr. Truman's veto statement.

Mitchell discussed the issue with Humphrey, who then wrote to Mrs. Rosenberg on October 16 stating that the section of the law she cited as requiring segregation actually was intended to safeguard standards of curriculum and staff, not to enforce segregation. Humphrey said he had been a member of the Senate labor committee that drafted the law and knew Congress' intent. This was a sharp change from Humphrey's statement in June that his "hands were tied" by the same law.

Hurried conferences were called at the Pentagon. Defense Department officials met with representatives of the Office of Education. Official correspondence shows that each agency refused to accept sole responsibility for racial policies at military post schools. Humphrey accused them of playing football with the issue and protested personally to Charles Murphy, one of Mr. Truman's legal advisers.

"I felt a moral obligation to do so," he said later. "I protested that the Defense Department and Office of Education were higgling and juggling the problem — and not deceiving anybody." He asked that responsibility be pinned down on one agency or the other.

The White House apparently thought so too. On January 10, 1953, Mrs. Rosenberg sought a showdown with Earl J. McGrath, U.S. Commissioner of Education. She wrote him saying that segregated army dependent schools at Forts Bliss, Sam Houston, Sill and Belvoir "do not result from a decision or discretion of the Department of Defense." She asked if he considered it "proper that children be required to attend a segregated school on a federal installation under a program financed to a considerable degree by federal money."

"It is our feeling that this practice is unsatisfactory and is violative not only of the new (non-segregation) policy of the Department of Defense but also contravenes the policy set forth by the President," she wrote.

McGrath replied on January 15, just five days before the Eisenhower administration was to take office. His answer, in essence, was that where the Office of Education ran schools on federal property, its aim was to follow the policies of the agency in control of the property.

"If it is the policy of the Department of Defense not to permit segregated education in any property within its control . . . this agency would, of course, be guided by such a policy." He said if local school authorities could not legally operate non-segregated schools on southern bases, the Office of Education would make "other arrangements" to teach the children.

This was a plain invitation to the Defense Department to state a policy of non-segregation in schools, with a promise that the Office of Education would carry it out.

There was no break in the developing policy when the Eisenhower administration took office. Dr. John A. Hannah, Michigan educator who succeeded Mrs. Rosenberg as Assistant Secretary of Defense for manpower, wrote to the Office of Education soon after he took office: "I . . . wish to assure you that the Department of Defense considers the integration of children attending such schools on military installations as a desirable goal."

On March 19 President Eisenhower, who had been briefed

on the military school picture before his inauguration, took a personal hand. He told a news conference, in answer to a reporter's question "planted" by Clarence Mitchell, that he would look into the military school problem. He said he did not see how any American could legally, logically or morally justify discrimination in use of federal funds.

Six days later the White House announced that segregation in all army schools wholly operated with federal funds would be ended by September [1953]. This actually applied only to Fort Benning, Georgia, which already had planned to begin the 1953-54 academic year with integrated schools.

The White House made public simultaneously a memorandum from Eisenhower to Secretary of Defense Charles E. Wilson, in which the President revealed that the Army was making a "survey" on the question of getting state and local governments to end segregation in post schools they operated.

"If such integration is not achieved, other arrangements in these instances will be considered," President Eisenhower said in the memo. His press secretary, James C. Hagerty, said "other arrangements" might mean additional federal expenditures to run non-segregated post schools.

The President's statement brought a sharp reaction from Governor Herman Talmadge of Georgia, who said Eisenhower had made a "great mistake." Fort Benning, however, took the White House announcement quietly. Some southern parents talked of sending their children to segregated off-base schools at their own expense. However, the school reopened in September on an integrated basis, and visiting Pentagon officers reported that the change took place without incident.

The Defense Department's school policy, which would govern all the U.S. military, appeared by the fall of 1953 to be crystallizing in this pattern:

All schools for children of military personnel located on military bases, whether federally or locally operated, would be unsegregated within the next year or two. Hannah named the 1955 fall term as the "target date" for ending the last segregation in post dependent schools. That would include Fort Bliss, whose segregation had prompted Mrs. Ferry's protest. If local agencies would not or could not operate unsegregated schools, the federal government would try to provide integrated schooling.

Some Pentagon officials were looking ahead to solving the problem of segregated education on southern bases which had no schools; children were sent to nearby communities and the costs defrayed by federal funds.

A proposed executive order was drafted in the Pentagon — but had not been approved at this writing — to direct that the government's standard non-discrimination clause be included in all contracts between the federal government and state agencies providing education for servicemen's children. If states refused, as those with segregation laws presumably must, the Office of Education would make other arrangements for non-segregated education of GIs' children. This would undoubtedly require more money to build additional on-post schools, and might lead to a fight in Congress over the issue.

Why the proposed order was held up was not entirely clear. There were indications that the Defense Department and Office of Education preferred to await the outcome of the Supreme Court's decision on the constitutionality of segregated public schools.

If the court outlawed segregated schools, there should be no need for the federal government to take steps of its own; although if some states carried out threats to abolish public schools, a fresh dilemma would be posed for the military.

But the military's successful racial integration program — particularly its smoothly functioning non-segregated schools — could temper the southern reaction to a Supreme Court decision against segregated education. Teachers like Mrs. Poole and the example of her integrated school might have a deep influence on public opinion far and near.

Mrs. Poole expressed her personal concern because, while children of both races went to the same elementary school at Fort Bragg, there was no base high school and older children had to attend segregated high schools off the base. She said she deliberately sent both Negro and white high school children on the same bus, which stopped first at the Negro high school, "to let them see, to give the white children the experience" of observing the southern cultural system and its "injustice" to the Negroes.

Perhaps the children, too, would have something to say in time.

TWENTY-TWO
Beyond Turning Back

What did the overall military racial pattern look like in August, 1953, at the conclusion of the Korean armistice and less than a decade after the Navy started its history-making racial experiment?

The Army, last to launch an all-out assault on segregation, had in three short years — starting in mid-1950 — switched from almost complete segregation to a point where better than nine out of every ten Negroes were serving in racially mixed units, according to official army figures.

Army troops throughout the Far East, in Korea and Japan, were totally unsegregated. Combat troops in Europe had wiped out racial separation, and service troops in Europe were nearing full integration, save for a number of all-Negro transportation and engineer units. In the continental United States, all basic training was free of racial barriers, and integration was largely complete in all the six regular army commands, as well as in the Alaskan Command.

In numbers, army figures showed that only about 10,000 Negroes were still serving in all-Negro units, out of some 200,000 Negroes in the entire Army, a tremendous shift in three years. More than half of the remaining Negro units were in Europe. Officials explained that it was difficult to break up all-Negro truck and engineer groups because there were few comparable white outfits to assimilate the Negroes. They figured this would be remedied in time by transfers and replacements; some estimated it might take up to two years or so for the elimination of remaining all-Negro units.[1]

Negroes numbered about 4,000 out of a total of some 114,000 army officers, the largest number and percentage of Negro officers in any service. Five Negroes were full colonels in August, 1953; senior among them was Colonel James H. Robinson, who had fought in North Africa and Italy, served in the Defense Department racial adviser's office and was Chief of the Labor Section on the staff of Lieutenant General Maxwell D. Taylor, commander of the U.S. Eighth Army in Korea, at the time of the Korean armistice.

The Air Force, which tackled full-scale integration before the Army, stated that its last all-Negro unit had been abolished by the end of 1952 and the 66,000 Negro airmen in service on August 1, 1953, were integrated among white units throughout the United States and overseas bases.

[1]Assistant Defense Secretary John A. Hannah said in an interview in *U.S. News and World Report,* released to the press October 12, 1953, that 95 percent of Negroes in the Army were then serving in unsegregated units. He said there would be no remaining segregated Army units eight months thence [June, 1954].

It listed 1,115 Negro officers out of an officer total of 124,462. Ninety-nine of the Negroes were majors, seven lieutenant colonels and four colonels. Colonel B. O. Davis, Jr., who until the spring of 1953 headed the Fighter Operations Branch in the Pentagon, was slated to command an F-86 Sabrejet wing in the Far East at the time of the Korean armistice and could become the second Negro general in United States history, the first having been his father, Brigadier General B. O. Davis.

The Marine Corps, last of the services to admit Negroes at all, reported that its last two all-Negro units — Marine barracks at naval ammunition depots — were integrated "some time" before the summer of 1952. A latecomer on the integration scene, the marines listed only about a dozen Negro officers in August, 1953, the highest with the rank of a first lieutenant.

Ironically, the Navy, which led the integration parade until 1949, was the chief target for criticism by Negro organizations in the summer of 1953, largely because of its remaining almost all-Negro Steward's Branch and its segregated facilities for civilian employees on some southern navy bases.

Of approximately 23,000 Negroes in the Navy in March, 1953, about one-half were in the Steward's Branch. The remaining Negroes in "general service" were scattered through nearly every job classification, from radio- and radarmen to signalmen, gunners, airplane pilots, mechanics, shore patrolmen and bookkeepers.

Negro officers in the Navy still were few. There were about ninety on active duty in August, 1953; the highest ranking was Lieutenant Commander Dennis D. Nelson II, son of a navy gunner aboard the battleship *Maine* and in turn father of a young naval officer, Ensign Dennis D. Nelson III, then serving aboard the Aircraft Carrier *Franklin D. Roosevelt;* a second Nelson son, Charles, was an Air Force officer trainee.

Despite the proportionately small number of Negro officers in all services, the number of Negroes graduated from the military and naval academies at West Point and Annapolis was slowly increasing. West Point was established in 1802 and the first Negro graduated in 1877; by 1942 only five Negroes had graduated; but seventeen graduated between then and 1953 and fourteen were in attendance during the 1950-51 school year. The first Negro to graduate from Annapolis was Ensign Wesley Brown in 1949; two more graduated in 1950 and 1952; there were five Negroes at Annapolis during the 1952-53 school year.

Negroes in all services totaled around 305,000 in August of 1953, approximately 8 1/2 percent of the military establishment. This compared to the Negro proportion of about 10 percent of the total U.S. population by latest Census Bureau estimates.

The official policy of the entire military establishment, enunciated during President Truman's administration and reaffirmed by his successor, President Eisenhower, was that segregation must be eliminated and "equality of treatment and opportunity" prevail for all.

Did military leaders truly agree that integration was the best way to handle racial problems, or were many of them secretly opposed?

Interviews with leading military and civilian officials in the defense establishment showed almost unanimous agreement that integration was fully accepted as the only way to use Negro manpower. These views were shared, among others, by Frank C. Pace, Jr., Arkansas-born Army Secretary during the Army's integration campaign; General Omar N. Bradley, a Missourian and Chairman of the U.S. Joint Chiefs of Staff until his retirement in August, 1953; Robert A. Lovett, a native Texan who was Secretary of Defense until the Eisenhower administration took office; General Hoyt S. Vandenberg, Air Force Chief of Staff until June 30, 1953; Lieutenant General Anthony C. McAuliffe, who moved from army personnel chief to Deputy Chief of Staff for Operations under the Eisenhower administration; Vice Admiral James L. Holloway, Jr., Chief of the Bureau of Naval Personnel in 1953; Lieutenant General Gerald C. Thomas, Chief of Staff of the Marine Corps in 1953; and James P. Mitchell, Assistant Secretary of Army for Manpower through most of 1953.

There was every indication that their views were shared by other military leaders in the Eisenhower administration, with the President himself setting the theme. Eisenhower had publicly supported continued army segregation in an appearance before the Senate Armed Services Committee on April 2, 1948, when various political groups, including some southern Democrats, looked to him as a possible presidential candidate. White House associates in 1953 pointed out that even then, however, Eisenhower had favored organizing Negroes "down to include units no larger than platoons," a view these associates described as being in advance of army racial policies at the time.

They depicted Eisenhower as believing social reform could accompany increased combat efficiency by progressive racial integration in the Army. No evidence had come to light at the time of this writing of any moves Eisenhower himself took to foster full-scale Army integration prior to his election to the presidency, though some officials said that when Eisenhower was Supreme Commander of North Atlantic Treaty forces in Europe his headquarters was "favorable" to non-segregation moves in U.S. Army forces in Europe.

After his election, Eisenhower took active steps to carry out his campaign pledge to end all remaining military segregation; he told a United Negro College Fund luncheon in Washington on May 9, 1953, that he "passionately" believed in equality, regardless of race or color, and that to the extent that there was recognition of "second class citizens," all others became less than first class.

Bradley, in an interview with this writer in 1953, said he had never doubted the "eventual desirability" of integration, but had worried "about pushing it before people were ready to accept it." He said all reports he had seen showed it "works fine in Korea." The only exceptions, he said, were statements by some regimental commanders that it might take time for Negro officers to be fully accepted as leaders of integrated units of company or battalion size.

Lovett said he was "sure integration will work if you don't force it; it's working as far as officers and ground troops are concerned; about pilots, I just don't know."

Vandenberg said that Negroes made "excellent airmen and pilots; if any aren't good, we get rid of them."

This author searched diligently for departures from this general agreement on the desirability of non-segregation; he found little among top-ranking military authorities. One "holdout" to whom he talked, a recently retired southern-born general with considerable experience in command of Negro troops, refused to be quoted by name but said bluntly he felt Negroes were not efficient fighters — segregated or integrated — and asserted that integration had been forced on the Army for political reasons.

He expressed the view that outstanding Negroes were exceptions and "you don't fight battles with exceptions"; he felt Negroes could be used effectively in artillery and service units but would "water down" combat forces.

"Americans," he declared, "are a different breed of cats from others. They have a sense of responsibility, pride, integrity, ability that the Negro does not possess. People think that being from the South we don't like Negroes. Not at all. But we understand their capabilities. And we don't want to sit at the table with them."

Asked if he thought integration would ever be abandoned, however, he replied, "No, I don't."

Another southern-born general, closely connected with the army's integration program, who remained in a high-ranking general staff post after the general quoted above had retired, was asked to comment on the contention that integration would lower the overall combat efficiency of the Army.

"Negroes in white companies do not weaken the Army to a definable extent," he said emphatically. "Nobody can show that they do. You can get opinions, yes, but facts, no!"

Little has been said about the marines thus far. They were part of the naval establishment and generally followed the Navy Department's lead. But the Marine Corps was in some ways the most striking example of racial alteration in the military services. Prior to 1942 there were literally no Negroes in the Corps, though marine historians said that a few were enrolled in the 19th century, chiefly young boys serving as musicians prior to 1835 and a few enlisted later as cooks and carpenters.

On May 20, 1942, following Secretary of the Navy Knox's order to open navy ratings to Negroes outside the Messman's Branch, a press release announced that the first battalion of some 900 Negro marines would be enlisted in June and July. An area known as Montford Point Camp at the Camp Lejeune, North Carolina, marine base was made ready to train the Negro marines. By mid-September, Colonel Samuel A. Woods, in command of the Negro contingent, reported that his recruits had shown "splendid aptitude for the service," and said he had "six probable rejections, but so far none of these has been for inaptitude."

With swelling enrollments from the draft, 19,168 Negro marines served during World War II, largely handling supplies and landing ammunition for invasions of Japanese-held islands in the Pacific. One ammunition company had the slogan, "You praise the Lord, we'll pass the ammunition." Ten Negro marines were killed in action, eighty-nine were wounded and two died of wounds in World War II.

Integration of Negro marines into white units was begun shortly after the war. Four of the six marine divisions were broken up and sent home, and the remaining two began integrating the Negroes who stayed in service. In July, 1949, Montford Point was closed as a separate training camp for Negroes. About the same time the last all-Negro fleet marine force — the marines' combat army — was integrated.

General Thomas, Chief of Staff and Assistant Commandant of the Marine Corps in August, 1953, said, "Integration of Negroes in the Marine Corps is here to stay; "colored boys are in almost every MOS (military occupational specialty) and certainly in every enlisted rank. I believe integration is satisfactory to them, and it is satisfactory to us."

Corps officials said that marine battalion commanders in Korea were almost unanimously favorable in reports on "integrated" Negroes in combat. One such battalion commander, a Medal of Honor winner from Georgia, said he had a number of Negroes in his outfit, which saw heavy fighting at the Chosin Reservoir in Korea; one all-white rifle platoon of forty-five men served under a Negro sergeant, and another twelve-man white squad was led by a Negro sergeant.

"There was no difference at all," he said. "I went on a patrol with the Negro squad leader; he was complete boss; there was no indication of any question but that he was well qualified."

This commander "never had much feeling" about Negroes despite his southern upbringing. "If a Negro were my executive officer, I would not mind sleeping in the same tent with him," he said.

TWENTY-THREE

Mop-up Campaign

Dwight D. Eisenhower, in his campaign for the presidency, promised to "end segregation" in the armed forces. Observers of the military scene knew how much had been done toward that end. They also were keenly aware of remaining areas of racial distinction.

Would the former five-star general, who once publicly supported continued segregation, take real steps to mop up remaining pools of segregation, they asked, or had he been merely playing the politician's game of "campaign promises?"

The answer soon became evident. On March 19 President Eisenhower told a news conference he did not approve of any discrimination in use of federal funds. Six days later he announced steps toward ending segregation in schools for servicemen's children on military posts. It would take time before results of these steps could be seen and measured. But in the Navy there were more direct results.

The Navy, under James Forrestal, had blazed the trail toward non-segregation. But in 1952 and early 1953, Negro leaders charged it was lagging behind the other services in finishing the job.

A memorandum, issued in January, 1952, under the direction of Navy Undersecretary Francis P. Whitehair, a Floridian, officially sanctioned use of segregated facilities for civilian workers in southern navy bases if that was the law, or custom, of nearby communities. Negro leaders called this a step backward, since at the time of its issuance the "white" and "Negro" signs on drinking fountains, rest rooms and other civilian facilities on southern bases had reportedly begun to disappear. It was reported that Negro sailors in uniform had been constrained to use the segregated facilities when in base civilian areas.

The Navy stood pat. Negro complaints reached the White House shortly before the Eisenhower administration took over. A few months later Representative Adam Clayton Powell, New York Negro congressman, raised the issue publicly, challenging the President to live up to his promises. The President sent the complaint to the Navy. From the new Navy Secretary, Robert B. Anderson, a Texan, came back another stand-pat reply, almost identical, word for word, with the last navy reply during the closing days of the Truman administration.

Powell sent Eisenhower an angry telegram on June 3, declaring that "your official family in the past five days has completely undermined your stated position on segregation." On June 9 the President replied to Powell, stating that "I will carry out every pledge I have made with regard to segregation." He added he had "made inquiries of the officials to whom you have referred," and "learned that they are pursuing the purpose of eliminating segregation in federally controlled and supported institutions."

Eisenhower did not mention the fact that, disturbed by Powell's charge, he had directed Maxwell M. Rabb, his White House minorities specialist, to tell Anderson of the President's strong belief that all military segregation must be ended. This Rabb did at a conference with Anderson and navy officials. Many of the officers insisted that the segregated facilities must be maintained or naval activities would be disrupted.

Anderson, according to one of those present, listened, then said he was inclined to go along with the President. He sent high-ranking officials to southern bases to work out plans to end the segregated facilities.

On August 20, following these visits, Anderson issued a press statement stating that he had made a survey which showed varying degrees of segregation in about half of the forty-two southern navy bases. He said commanders concerned had been "requested to proceed steadily and expeditiously" toward ending "all barriers to the free use of facilities. . . ."

The following day the United Press, in a dispatch from Washington, quoted high-ranking admirals, including the commander of the Norfolk base, as declaring they would not act without written orders. The story caused a minor explosion within the Navy. Day-long conferences were held at which Anderson made it plain he meant what he said. That evening letters went out to all southern navy bases stating Anderson had "directed" that they "proceed steadily" to eliminate the segregated facilities.

Commanders promptly posted orders in the southern bases complying with their written instructions. The Charleston base removed racial signs from drinking fountains in September, and listed segregation in cafeterias and rest rooms as next to go. A report from Negro workers at the Norfolk Navy Base to the Washington office of the NAACP said the "walls are coming down all over" the base. There were similar reports from other bases.

Anderson called for progress reports every sixty days, the first due November 1. He told this writer in September that if insufficient progress were reported, he would take steps to speed action. He stressed that he wanted the goal accomplished without incident and without discredit to officers involved.

Negro leaders, who had eyed the navy chief from Texas suspiciously, were surprised and delighted. One of these was Lester Granger, head of the National Urban League, who had been approached early in 1953 to serve as a part time racial consultant to the Navy, a role he had performed for Forrestal. Granger requested advance assurance that the Navy would take positive steps toward ending its civilian segregation, changing the Negro character of its Steward's Branch, and increasing the number of Negro officers.

Failing at first to get such assurances, Granger wrote friends he could only assume the Navy had no intention of acting, and prepared to denounce navy race practices at a September meeting of the Urban League.

On September 3, Anderson held a luncheon at the Pentagon for Granger. Present, in addition to the Secretary, were the top officers concerned with civilian and naval personnel; three retired navy officers who had worked with Forrestal on the early integration program; and James C. Evans, Defense Department racial adviser.

In the presence of this audience, Anderson announced his new policy on civilian employees. He went on to say that his goal was complete integration of Negroes in the Navy. He said he wanted to move as fast as possible, with precautions against incidents that might retard progress. He added he would consider it a "feather in my cap" if he could list elimination of all remaining racial barriers as an accomplishment of his administration.

Shortly after the luncheon Anderson told this author he had asked Vice Admiral James L. Holloway, Jr., Chief of Naval Personnel, to begin studies aimed at integrating the Negro Steward's Branch. He said he was going to look into the question of securing more Negro officers in the Navy. He said, "I am setting up as an objective the elimination of segregation in all areas where the government owns the facilities, among civilians as well as uniformed personnel. I'd consider it one of the rewarding accomplishments of my administration if I could eliminate all barriers to complete integration without reflection on those of any race in the Navy."

He acknowledged that his earlier reply to Powell's complaint was a mistake; due to his lack of familiarity with circumstances, he had merely passed along a statement written by his subordinates. Asked why he, a Texan, supported non-segregation in the Navy, Anderson replied simply, "I have no bias or prejudice of any kind."

While the Navy was thus caught in the spotlight of publicity, Assistant Army Secretary James P. Mitchell quietly checked on army bases in the South and found many similar segregated civilian facilities in existence. Avoiding public attention, he quietly called together officials in charge of activities at southern army bases and told them to get rid of the segregation as fast as possible. He issued no directives or written orders but made it plain he wanted action. At the time of this writing, the Army was reported moving even faster than the Navy toward eliminating its segregated civilian facilities.

In both the army and navy moves, racial experts in the Pentagon noted with satisfaction the result they had come to expect in steps to end segregation — no untoward incidents or trouble of any kind.

Negro leaders had other complaints about the armed services in 1953. They continued critical of the Army for not eliminating its remaining all-Negro units, though part of this criticism was admittedly based on lack of information as to how far the Army had gone. When the news broke in October that 95 percent of army Negroes were serving in integrated units, one Negro leader exclaimed, "That's wonderful!"

Other complaints centered around the continued use of racial designations on individual soldiers' travel orders, and on other military forms and reports. If there were no discrimination or segregation, there would be no need for such racial labels, some Negro leaders maintained.

Military officials defended the maintenance of racial tags. Denying discrimination was involved, they said such designations were needed to supply information to Congress, the press and the public, and to make sure the integration program was enforced. Pentagon racial advisers, who looked forward to the eventual elimination of such labels, did not then consider their continued existence discriminatory.

Negro spokesmen pointed to other aspects of the military picture they still regarded as unsatisfactory in August, 1953. They said most state National Guard units still were segregated; and they reported complaints from Negroes unable to get into military reserve forces in some states, or not assigned to reserve posts merited by their previous service.

Besides objection to segregated schooling, remaining criticism of military race policy from anti-segregation spokesmen was based largely on less general practices. Cases were reported in which Negro officers were denied housing in projects under military control. Contracts were signed with southern colleges to provide extension classes for servicemen, though the colleges barred Negroes; alternate arrangements for Negroes to take similar courses on the base did not prove satisfactory.

There were still officers in all services who resented the presence of Negroes and tried to limit their opportunities for equal treatment and promotion; though as far as could be learned such cases, when fully substantiated and brought to the attention of proper authorities, were almost always corrected in the end. It was this author's observation that nearly all officials in positions of authority in the headquarters of all services were opposed to such forms of discrimination.

One aspect of military integration, touched on but briefly here, was the status of civilian employees of the military. Roughly half the two and a half million civilians working for the federal government were employed by the armed services in 1953. While there was no segregation in jobs as such, Negroes seldom were advanced beyond the $3,500-a-year level which largely covered jobs such as stenographers, file clerks, messengers and similar positions. Pentagon racial specialists considered it incongruous for military integration to exist side by side with these racial differentials among civilians supporting the military, and had begun work on the problem.

A final consideration in the military racial picture, which had troubled military leaders for years, was the question of quotas. Many military leaders expressed fear, as recently as 1953, that the armed forces would take in far more Negroes than the proportion in the total population. While there was no publicly acknowledged objection to this, many senior officers said frankly in private that such a development would frustrate one of the major aims of the integration program by restoring the "bunching" of Negroes they considered one of the evils of segregation.

No official quotas existed in any service in 1953, and branches other than the Army had less concern since their Negro percentages were well below the level of the general population. Some army authorities were disturbed about their Negro strength, which had reached 13 percent of total army strength in August, 1953.[1] However, army-hired research experts had reported earlier that there was little prospect in the foreseeable future that the Army's Negro contingent would rise above 15 percent. These experts, and racial specialists in the Pentagon, agreed that any substantial rise above that level could, if desired, be countered effectively by raising minimum mental standards for army admission. This would automatically exclude a greater proportion of Negroes as long as the Negro educational level remained below that of whites.

Summing up the feeling of militant anti-segregationists about the military situation in August, 1953, a spokesman for a leading Negro organization told this writer, "It is still short of what it should be, and our files have many complaints; a commander at some base will not enforce the non-segregation policy; Negro servicemen traveling with whites will be fed in the kitchen of some southern restaurant while the whites eat in the dining room.

"But the facts warrant a feeling that a lot of progress has been made. I would not have dreamed it possible ten years ago."

[1] In August, 1953, Negroes constituted 6.98 percent of the Air Force, 6.6 percent of the Marine Corps and a little over 3.5 percent of the Navy.

TWENTY-FOUR
Unbunching — A New Concept

Before the military men and their civilian bosses took the new racial road, vast and far-reaching changes were under way throughout the United States, and they continued thereafter with accelerating motion.

Segregation barriers were crumbling, more here, less there, but inexorably. In education, housing, employment, public accommodation and other aspects of life, American Negroes had made gains toward equality of treatment that Negro leaders called "remarkably good" compared with conditions twenty years ago.

A glance at news stories in 1953 told a graphic story:

"Phoenix, Ariz., July 15 (UP)—School officials today predicted 'complete integration' of grade school classes here by September, 1954."

197

"Atlanta, May 14, (UP)—A Negro educator who became the first of his race to defeat a white man at the polls here in this century said today his victory means southerners are 'far ahead of what some people think.'"

"Washington, D. C., June 9—(*The Washington Post*)— "It is unlawful for Washington restaurants to deny service to any persons because of their race, the Supreme Court ruled yesterday."

"Atlanta, June 21 (UP)—Hiram W. Evans, national leader of the Ku Klux Klan in its prime, said today that the hooded order 'is practically extinct . . . and there's little need for it anyway . . . we are pretty well united and we have a good president.'"

"New Orleans, Nov. 18 (1952) (UP)—The Southern Governors' Conference elected Georgia Gov. Herman Talmadge, a staunch proponent of racial segregation, as its chairman today and then heard a speaker say the end of segregation is 'sure to come' eventually."

Almost daily, new Negro "firsts" could be found. The first Negro woman was named "Mother of the Year" by white clubwomen in Virginia; the first Negro state cabinet member was appointed in Illinois; for the first time a Negro was made a member of a medical society in Virginia.

There were still vast areas of segregation and discrimination in civilian life, particularly in the South. But lynchings, one barometer of racial antagonisms, had died almost to nothing, and instances of acceptance of Negroes in public places were increasing steadily.

In this movement the military acted as a catalyst, speeding up the slow process of racial change to an immeasurable degree. Military leaders, often considered impervious to change, had seized the initiative and paced the rest of the nation in this major alteration of a social pattern.

While most professional military men had stressed military efficiency as their chief motivation, their civilian leaders —

Harry Truman, Stuart Symington, James Forrestal, Frank Pace, Earl Johnson — were prompted likewise by strong democratic principles, frequently by religious and moral considerations.

How had the military acted as a spearhead toward nonsegregation throughout the United States as a whole?

First, by power of example. By knocking down its racial barriers, the military had shown it could be done; that Negroes and whites, despite a long history of sharp separation and frequently deep-seated antagonism, would work, live and play together with little or no concern once they got used to the idea.

Secondly, there was no way to bottle up racial integration within military precincts. Men leaving service were taking back to civilian life at least some of their new experience. Part might "wear off" among men returning to rigidly segregated communities; some might have acquired or increased a dislike of Negroes in service and retained this attitude afterward; but from all available evidence the great majority of men in integrated units took home a fresh slant on race free from the basic concept of segregation that once dominated the American scene. This type of experience was certain to influence not only the men themselves but also their families, friends and casual acquaintances.

A third impact was in direct military contacts with outside communities. Integration was spilling over uncontrollably. Churches, USO clubs, cafes and taxicabs, in the North and South, here and there began voluntarily to admit Negroes on an equal or near-equal basis with white servicemen. But could the military avoid *direct* intervention at times, despite its basic policy of non-interference with civilian customs? The impracticality of providing separate housing and restaurants for Negroes in towns with virtually no Negro populations had demonstrated the need for military pressure on behalf of Negro servicemen's families.

Then, too, there were instances of actual interference with local racial practices. Military files recorded that the provost marshal on one northern post told a nearby bar owner to serve all soldiers or his cafe would be put off limits; the bar owner agreed to serve a Negro soldier who had complained. An entertainment officer at another base found that a matron in charge of rounding up girls for post dances objected to white girls riding in the same bus with Negro girls. The officer ordered the bus driver to pick up the Negro girls and leave the whites behind. Another hostess soon was obtained who did not object to sharing the bus.

Racial experts in the Pentagon told this writer that, despite the military's policy of non-interference in outside civilian life, there was a serious morale problem involved in instances of off-post racial discrimination involving servicemen.

The Army's research teams pinpointed this factor in two interviews. One was with a Negro private who told of walking past a restaurant and seeing Negro and white GI's seated together at a table inside. He said it "made me feel equal to the others, that I had something to fight for, that I, too, was an American."

But another Negro private related how he went into a downtown restaurant with two white friends, only to be told, "We don't serve colored here."

"It definitely lowers a soldier's morale," said the Negro. "Those are the type of incidents that make Paul Robeson's arguments weighty."

What, if anything, could civilians who are interested in removing racial barriers learn from the military accomplishment? Obviously it was impossible to try by decree to alter the long established folkways of American civilians. Military men readily acknowledged the big part that military discipline — the habit of accepting orders, no matter how seemingly unreasonable — has had in the successful removal of military segregation. Whether or not some of the techniques used in the armed forces could be useful as guides to civilian agencies seeking to tackle racial problems remained to be seen.

An air staff officer said that racial difficulties occurred where Negroes were massed together. "I always felt it was a mistake to mass them in large groups, in cities or in the services," he said. "You get riots when Negroes are massed. When they are spread, they mix in, according to their ability."

Some men within the military establishment, looking even beyond the American framework, were beginning to wonder if the "unbunching" or "integration" concept might some day have a place in removing international antagonism where guns and armies fail.

A high civilian official of the Air Force's Air Training Command commented that his command had recently integrated foreign military students, here to learn American military methods, with U.S. airmen, where they had been kept separate before. This was done deliberately, to teach mutual understanding and friendship between American airmen and their allies.

The official went on to say, "If we had some way of mixing the American and Russian people together, integrating them, some of the culture of both would rub off, and maybe it would end all this mess."

Perhaps the U.S. military integration indicated a growing awareness of the need to cultivate man's human relationships — with friend and potential foe alike.

Brigadier General Lloyd Hopwood, deputy chief of Air Force

personnel, seemed to touch this note when he stopped one day to talk with the author, who was examining letters from Air Force commanders attesting the smooth success of the Air Force integration program.

"I like to go through them myself once in a while," the busy military leader said. "It kind of restores my faith in human nature."

Bibliography

Williams, George W.: *A History of the Negro Troops in the War of the Rebellion 1861-1865,* Harper & Brothers, New York, 1888.

Cashin, Herschel V.; Alexander, Charles; Anderson, William T.; Brown, Arthur M.; Bivins, Horace W.: *Under Fire with the Tenth U.S. Cavalry,* F. Tennyson Neely, New York, 1899.

Scott, Emmett J.: *Scott's Official History of the American Negro in the World War,* copyright 1919 by Scott. Copy obtained in Library of Congress; no indication of publisher.

Little, Arthur W.: *From Harlem to the Rhine,* Covici Friede, New York, 1936.

Nelson, Dennis Denmark, Lt. USNR: *The Integration of the Negro into the U.S. Navy 1776-1947,* monograph from thesis of same title submitted to Department of Sociology, Howard University, 1948; Navy Department imprint.

Wiley, Bell Irvin: *Southern Negroes 1861-1865,* Yale University Press, New Haven, 1938.

Franklin, John Hope: *From Slavery to Freedom,* A. A. Knopf, New York, 1947.

Report of the Gillem Board, War Department, November 17, 1945, in the form of a memorandum to the Chief of Staff.

War of the Rebellion, Official Records of the Union and Confederate Armies, War Department. Series I, Volume 46, Part 2.

Bancroft, George: *History of the United States of America, from the Discovery of the Continent;* Author's Last Revision; D. Appleton and Company, New York, 1887.

A Study of the Negro in Military Service, by Jean Byers, June, 1947; mimeographed copy "reproduced for [defense] departmental use, January, 1950. Foreword by James C. Evans, Civilian Assistant to the Secretary of Defense, states work is based on "departmental records, historical materials, and press reports of the period of World War II."

A Fragment of Victory in Italy during World War II, 1942-45, a Special Study of the 92nd Infantry Division, prepared at the Army War College by Maj. Paul Goodman, Artillery, Staff and Faculty.

The Colored Soldier in the U.S. Army, prepared in the Historical Section, Army War College, May, 1942 (in the form of a memorandum for Col. Ralph L. Tate, office of the Assistant Secretary of War).

White, Walter, *A Man Called White,* The Viking Press, New York, 1948.

U.S. Naval Administration in World War II, Bureau of Naval Personnel; subtitle, The Negro in the Navy; Draft Narrative prepared under the general supervision of the Director of Naval History, Adm. E. C. Kalbfus, retired.

Abraham Lincoln, His Speeches and Writings, edited by Roy P.

Basler, The World Publishing Co., Cleveland and New York, 1946.

Arnold, Samuel Greene: *History of the State of Rhode Island and Providence Plantations,* D. Appleton & Co., London and New York, 1859-60 (2 vols.).

Index

A

Acheson, Dean 49, 57, 155

Advance and Retreat 24

Air Force, U. S. 6, 10, 18, 43, 46, 47, 65, 67, 68, 69, 70, 71, 72, 81, 82, 85, 88, 89, 90, 93, 94, 95, 96, 105, 121, 125, 126, 127, 133, 139, 140, 141, 149, 150, 151, 163, 165, 167, 168, 169, 181, 184, 196, 201, 202

Air Proving Ground Headquarters 90

Air University 46

Almond, Edward M., 14

Allen, Major General Terry de la Mesa 62

Amarillo Air Base 151

American, Dilemma, An (Myrdal) 42

Anderson, Jean S. 54

Anderson, Robert B. 190

Army, U.S. 5, 6, 7, 10, 12, 13, 15, 16, 17, 21, 23, 24, 25, 34, 35, 37, 38, 39, 41, 42, 43, 45, 59, 62, 63, 66, 67, 69, 71, 77, 82, 83, 84, 85, 86, 87, 96, 97, 98, 99, 100, 101, 102, 103, 104, 105, 109, 110, 111, 112, 113, 114, 115, 117, 118, 120, 121, 123, 124, 125, 130, 131, 151, 159, 165, 166, 167, 170, 177, 180, 181, 183, 184, 185, 186, 193, 194, 196, 200

Army War College 12, 21, 30, 32, 64, 204

Attucks, Crispus 20

B

Baker, Newton D. 29

Basler, Roy P. 162, 204

Baumann, Paul F. 139

Benjamin O. Davis 42, 59, 89–95

Benton, William H. 122

Biggs Field 95

Bingham, Lieutenant Colonel Dwight 129

T

Talmadge, Herman 177, 198
Taylor, First Lieutenant Jack 140
Taylor, Lieutenant General Maxwell D. 181
Thomas, Lieutenant General Gerald C. 184, 187
Thompson, Worthington 83
Time Magazine 44
Trud (Soviet magazine) 155
Truman, Harry S., 10, 11, 66, 68, 70, 73, 74, 75, 76, 77, 78, 80, 81, 87, 97, 154, 173, 174, 175, 183, 199
Truscott, Lieutenant General Lucien D. 15
Tuskegee Institute 40, 41, 42, 43, 45, 68, 71, 74
Twining, Major General Nathan F. 46

U

Ulvert M. Moore 53
United Negro College Fund 185
United Press 191
U. S. Military Academy (West Point) 42, 157, 183
U. S. Naval Academy (Annapolis) 183

V

Van Ness, Lieutenant Commander D. 51
Vandenberg, General Hoyt S. 70, 71, 72, 184, 185

W

Walker, Lieutenant General Walton H. 18, 101
War Department, U. S. 12, 14, 28, 29, 34, 35, 38, 39, 43, 61, 63, 66, 68, 76, 204
War Manpower Commission 51
Washington, Booker T. 30
Washington, George 21
Washington Post 26, 84, 198
Watley, Colonel Vachel D., Jr. 129
Watson, Technical Sergeant James A. 134
Weaver, George L. P. 152
Wetzel, Earl 147
White, Dale L. 73
White, Walter 34, 35, 66
Whitehair, Francis P. 190
Wiley, Bell I. 24
Willkie, Wendell 49
Wilson, Charles E. 66, 177
Wolcott, Major John P. 147
Woods, Colonel Samuel A. 186
Woodward, Isaac 65
Wynn, Lieutenant Ellison C. 106

Y

Young, Private First Class Donald T. 5

Z

Zuckert, Eugene 68, 69, 70

PHOTO SECTION

Ensign Jesse L. Brown/U.S. Navy: 1949 (One of the First Black Officers in the "New" Navy).

A

Breakthrough on the Color Front

EXTENSION OF REMARKS
OF

HON. HUBERT H. HUMPHREY

OF MINNESOTA

IN THE SENATE OF THE UNITED STATES

Saturday, April 18, 1953

Mr. HUMPHREY. Mr. President, I ask unanimous consent that an article by Mr. Lee Nichols, a United Press correspondent attached to the Washington office of that news-service organization, be printed in the Appendix of the RECORD.

The article, Breakthrough on the Color Front, appears in the April 6, 1953, issue of the Freeman. It is a splendid presentation of the progress we have been making as a nation in eliminating segregation in our Armed Forces. Mr. Nichols has made an extensive study of this problem. I am pleased that he is currently at work on a book about race relations in the armed services. I am certain that it will be a fine contribution and I am looking forward with great interest to reading it. I recommend Mr. Nichol's article to the attention of the Senate.

There being no objection, the article was ordered to be printed in the RECORD, as follows:

BREAKTHROUGH ON THE COLOR FRONT

(By Lee Nichols)

A recently-captured Russian propaganda film purports to show a Negro soldier being kicked out of a GI club for daring to enter and ask for a beer. Distributed among ker races of the world, it is part of a growing Soviet campaign to prove the United States hates nonwhites.

But recently, as I was having a drink at a GI club at Camp Lejeune in North Carolina, a Negro marine sergeant walked in, checked his cap, and ordered a whiskey. Sipping it, he struck up a casual conversation with me and another white man. Nobody turned a hair. Later, as we played billiards, a white GI waiter asked the sergeant in a southern drawl, "May I get you something, sir?"

I asked the Negro how he was getting along in the Marine Corps, which, 10 years ago, bristled at the very thought of a colored leatherneck.

"Fine," he replied. "There's no segregation here. We work and eat together, and sleep in the same barracks. I've learned to like a lot of white people, and I've been given no reason to think they don't approve of me."

The incident spotlights a silent, but successful, revolution that has taken place in the Armed Forces. It is a revolution that will help crumble racial walls in the United States, and could tip the scales for victory in another war.

At the start of World War II, Negroes were second-class soldiers. They could join the Navy, but only as stewards. They couldn't get into the Marines, or fly in the Army Air Corps. The Army had four all-Negro regiments which, though combat-trained had many of their men used as orderlies and grooms.

Today the picture is totally different. Col. Benjamin O. Davis, Jr., a Negro officer, is responsible for fighter-plane tactics for the entire Air Force. He commands white subordinates at the Pentagon and lunches with white officers daily.

Sgt. Cornelius H. Charlton, 21-year-old Negro from New York City, was fighting with his Army platoon in Korea. When his white lieutenant fell, Charlton took over. He led an attack on a steep hill, personally wiping out two enemy positions with rifle and grenades before dying of his own wounds. He was awarded the Congressional Medal of Honor—one of the two Army Negroes to get this top honor in the Korean War to date. No Negro won it in World Wars I or II.

The military has played its cards close to its chest, and the public is still mostly unaware of the aboutface on colored troops. Here are the facts:

The Air Force has no remaining all-Negro units. Negro airmen are battling MIG's in Korea, instructing jet pilots in Arizona, servicing intercontinental bombers in England. At Ellington Air Force base, in Texas, a football game was scheduled with a nearby town. Town officials asked that Negroes on the Air Force team be barred. Instead, Col. Benjamin T. Starkey, base commander, canceled the game. He reported: "All members of the team concurred wholeheartedly."

The Army has moved more cautiously. But it has erased the color line wherever United States troops are serving in the Far East, is swiftly following suit in Germany and other overseas areas, and is steadily moving toward the same goal at home. Racial intergration is complete at all 10 training bases, some in the deep South, at all officer and technical schools, and to varying degrees in the 3 regular combat divisions stationed in the United States.

SIDE BY SIDE

I visited the Fort Jackson Infantry Training Center at Columbia, S. C. In its sprawling barracks, I watched white boys from Mississippi cleaning their rifles next to Negroes from Louisiana. I saw them swimming together in the same pool, sitting side by side in the post movie.

At Fort Bragg, N. C., I stood beside Maj. Gen. Charles D. W. Canham, boss of the 82d Airborne Division, watching Negro and white paratroopers filing abroad a transport plane.

"These colored boys are really sharp," he shouted above the plane's roar. "They keep the white boys on their toes, and they're not afraid to jump."

Col. Robert Luckey, chief of staff at Camp Lejeune, told me: "Negroes make good marines. If a marine's a rifleman, he goes to a rifle company, regardless of color; a radarman goes to a radar outfit. Children of our colored marines go to the base school with

B

white kids. There's no difference."

The Navy lays claim to trailblazing this road by putting whites and Negroes together on ships in 1944. A Virginia-born engineer who was aboard a Navy tanker in those days recalled the first colored fireman assigned to his department. "We told him he must have come to the wrong place," he said. "It seemed pretty strange, but we got along. We slept in the same compartment."

About 50 percent of the Navy's Negroes are still in the racially distinct stewards' branch, but the die is cast. Today Negro bluejackets are doing practically every job handled by white sailors. They eat and bunk together, drink beer with white shipmates at Navy canteens ashore.

NO MORE SECOND-CLASS SOLDIERS

Negro soldiers and sailors date back to the Revolutionary War, when slaves and freedmen fought the British side by side with white patriots. When the Civil War came, however, a color line was drawn that lasted through World War II. Though Negro battalions chalked up heroic achievements, they were most remembered for their failures. One regiment went to pieces under attack in World War I, causing commanders to say scornfully, "The Negro is too emotional to fight a war." "I saw them run," an officer told me of colored soldiers in World War II. Poorly trained officers and bad morale, due to discrimination, helped create the failures. Today military planners are convinced that Negroes kept apart as second-class soldiers make second-class fighters.

Late in World War II, James Forrestal, then Secretary of the Navy, decided to try an experiment. In private life he had been a contributor to racial-improvement groups and knew that Negroes were rapidly gaining in education and skills. Their manpower was sorely needed, so Forrestal insisted that the Navy try mixing Negroes in crews of transports and other auxiliary ships. "They're good sailors," said a white ship captain.

On February 27, 1946, Forrestal ordered the entire Navy opened to Negroes—all jobs, all ships, all bases. It was only a matter of time before the whole military began picking it up. The military's about face was executed through stern necessity—plus the fact that, when tried, it worked.

W. STUART SYMINGTON, first Secretary of the independent Air Force, took the next step. The old Army Air Corps had finally let Negroes fly in World War II, but trained by themselves and kept in all-Negro squadrons. After the war, there were so many Negro pilots, navigators, and other specialists, the Air Force didn't know what to do with them. But white air units were woefully short of skilled men.

SYMINGTON talked with Forrestal. "Shove 'em all together," was his conclusion. The all-Negro wing at Lockbourne Field, Ohio, was broken up, its airmen sprinkled among bases worldwide.

President Truman pushed the movement along. On July 26, 1948, he issued an Executive order providing for "equality of treatment and opportunity for all persons in the armed services without regard to race, color, religion, or national origin." He also set up a civilian committee, headed by Georgia-born Judge Charles Fahy, to see it was carried out.

The Fahy committee found that all-Negro Army outfits could not, of themselves, absorb the potential skills of colored soldiers. This tended to keep Negroes out of the service's specialist schools. The Army agreed this was unfair. In January 1950 Secretary Gordon Gray authorized the use of Negroes in any outfit where their skills were needed. This opened the technical schools to them.

But it was the Korean war that gave the change real impetus. It was wasteful to build up two sets of training camps when the need was for speed. And at the front, white units were being decimated, while behind the lines all-Negro outfits—which were thought not to measure up in combat—were over strength.

"Let me mix them in," pleaded Gen. Matthew Ridgway. "Go ahead," said the Pentagon. Soon Negro soldiers were bivouacking with whites at Kumhwa, fighting shoulder to shoulder at Capitol Hill and Sniper Ridge.

"HE SAVED MY LIFE"

Pvt. Donald Young, of Roanoke, Va., 24, white, crouched in his bunker atop Capitol Hill one night as the North Koreans were attacking. A grenade thudded into the bunker. He tried to kick it out but it exploded under his foot. "Medic," he screamed, but no one came. Painfully he crawled to the next bunker. There in the darkness, himself under fire, his squad leader, a Negro sergeant, tied a tourniquet on the mangled leg, untwisting it at intervals to restore circulation. Two hours passed. The attack was beaten off. Young was flown back to the United States, his leg off below the knee.

I talked with Young at Walter Reed Hospital in Washington, D. C., where he was waiting to be fitted with an artificial foot. I asked if he expected to see his sergeant again.

"He can come to my home any time he wants to," Young replied. "Wouldn't that upset his southern neighbors?" I asked. "Maybe so," he said. "But he saved my life. He's as good a man as I am."

Late in 1951, the Army sent teams of social scientists to Korea, and bases in the United States, to check the effects of racial mixing. They brought back three thick volumes of some of the most important racial findings ever made—evidence that men of different races can get along in time of stress.

Among white officers quizzed in Korea, 9 out of 10 rated integrated units equal to, or better than all-white units in morale, teamwork, and aggressiveness in battle. Here are some typical questions asked of the officers:

"In hand-to-hand combat can you depend on the Negro soldier in an integrated unit to hold his ground better than, not as well as, or about the same as the white soldier? (Check one)." Two-thirds checked "about the same."

"In an integrated unit do the Negro soldiers maintain their weapons in good condition better than, less well, or about as well as white soldiers in combat? (Check one.)" Nine out of 10 checked "about as well."

Reprinted in Readers Digest sometime in 1953.

B'

New York Post

Weekly Book Reviews

News (Good News) About the Negro in The Armed Forces

LEE NICHOLS

BREAKTHROUGH ON THE COLOR FRONT. By Lee Nichols. Random. 235 pp. $3.50

By TED POSTON

This quietly dramatic little book is going to shock a lot of Americans. But happily for the increasingly adult nation to which it is addressed, it may elate more Americans than it shocks.

For "Breakthrough on the Color Front" unveils one of the best-kept secrets of the last decade—the rapid and almost complete integration of the Negro into the country's armed forces. And, as the author claims, it may well turn out to be "one of the biggest stories of the 20th Century." Surely one of the most significant.

Bits and pieces of the story have leaked out here and there, many of them reported by Lee Nichols, a rewrite man on the night desk of United Press in Washington.

* * *

But probably only two groups knew the real extent of the almost incredible social change wrought in our military structure over the last decade—and each kept quiet about it for its own reasons.

The National Assn. for the Advancement of Colored People, which has spearheaded the drive for complete equality in the a[illegible]ed forces, was determined to bestow no bouquets on the military until the full goal was in sight.

And the military, no little bit astounded at the rapidity of its own progress, kept quiet for fear that Congress and recalcitrant elements in its own ranks might try to bring back the days of ... racial tensions

Best Sellers (In New York)

FICTION

1. **Lord Vanity — Shellabarger**
2. **Not as a Stranger—Thompson**
3. **Time and Time Again—Hilton**
4. **Beyond This Place—Cronin**
5. **Battle Cry—Uris**

NON-FICTION

1. **Life Is Worth Living—Sheen**
2. **The Power of Positive Thinking—Peale**
3. **Triumph and Tragedy—Churchill**
4. **Fire in the Ashes—White**
5. **Second Tree From the Corner—White**

Air Force; that only 10,000 of the 200,000 Negroes in the Army still serve in all-Negro units; that with the exception of its still segregated Stewards' Branch, the Navy has scattered the remainder of its 23,000 Negro bluejackets into almost every category from radioman to airplane pilot. And that the Marine Corps, the last of the services to admit Negroes, abolished its last two all-Negro units in the spring of 1952.

Others will be shocked—or elated—to learn that Negro and white servicemen are now eating, sleeping, working and playing together at all Southern military establishments; that several white churches there encourage Negro soldiers and airmen to attend their services; that many Southern communities, from Biloxi, Miss., to Brownsville, Tex., have altered their tradi- ... Jim Crow practices to ...

throughout the world, Negroes and white servicemen stationed there are completely integrated—to the consternation ofttimes of our Communist critics.

* * *

The drama of this book lies in Nichols' well-documented story of how and why this was accomplished, and in the part played by many big and little people in breaking down the tradition-crusted brass and loud-mouthed politicians who opposed it.

The "why" is simple, but it took the military a long time to see it. You can't create a fighting man by treating him as a pariah; you can't create a fighting machine when many of its components are not meshed and are not regarded as really important to the operation.

* * *

Many big men of vision knew this and were unrelenting in the fight—men like Franklin D. Roosevelt, James V. Forrestal and Stuart Symington. And none knew it better or did more about it than a stubborn little fellow from Missouri who had seen the "why" demonstrated on battlefields of France in World War I—chap by name of Harry S. Truman.

And although as late as 1948 he was still fighting for the maintenance of Jim Crow in the U. S. Army, President Eisenhower—in this instance at least—has carried on the banner first h... ...decessors.

... has been so ...se Secre-

COPY

NATIONAL URBAN LEAGUE
INCORPORATED
NEW YORK. N. Y.

June 2, 1954

Mr. James C. Evans
Civilian Assistant
Office of the Assistant Secretary
 of Defense
Washington 25, D. C.

Dear Jim:

Believe it or not, I'm just now getting down to that
place in my stack of unanswered mail where your letter
of March 30th has rested, asking for a statement on
Lee Nichols' work.

I enjoyed reading Lee Nichols' "Break-through On The
Color Front" from start to finish, for several reasons.
It is well written and immensely readable. It is closely
documented. Its coverage is broader than that of any
previous volume on the subject. It includes the human
interest part of the story by going into personalities
and motives, as well as facts and figures. Lee Nichols
has made a tremendous contribution to the whole movement of interracial integration.

Sincerely,

Lester B. Granger
Executive Director

LBG:cs

D

Fashioned In Battle

BREAKTHROUGH ON THE COLOR FRONT. By Lee Nichols. 235 pp. New York: Random House. $3.50.

By S. L. A. MARSHALL

Pilots of the 8th Fighter Bomber Wing at a briefing in Korea, January, 1953.

BY producing a first-class study of a major problem in American race relationships Lee Nichols, who works the night desk for The United Press in Washington, has demonstrated that any time a good reporter aspires to write a book he will find rich material kicking around underfoot.

Some months ago he read a casual press release from the Pentagon which put him on the trail of what he calls "one of the biggest stories of the twentieth century." Potentially it warrants no lesser description. He followed it through the bureaus, reading staff papers and interviewing hundreds of officials until he had collected most of the main facts. His book tells how, under the pressures of the Korean war, the United States armed establishment, almost unnoticed, achieved the long-awaited reform and made an end to military race segregation.

Also, to measure the significance of this unheralded victory, the reporter turned historian. How things stand today —and except for a few marginal discriminations which will shortly pass the services now adhere to a standard of equal treatment—is profiled against the prolonged struggle toward that object.

Mr. Nichols traces the long story of the Negro's participation in the American armed forces from that day in 1770 when the Negro Crispus Attucks was the first person shot and one of five killed at the Boston Massacre that preceded the Revolution. Negroes fought in all our wars, he reminds us— the Revolution, War of 1812, Civil War, Spanish-American and both world wars. And he shows how in these conflicts and the peacetime years between Negroes made slow but steady progress toward full integration in Army, Navy and Air Force. An important factor in the advance was President Truman's Committee on Equality of Treatment and Opportunity in the Armed Services.

BY 1953, Mr. Nichols says, "The racial barrier had been virtually wiped out in the Air Force and in the Navy outside the almost entirely Negro Steward's Branch. The Army was far along the road to elimination of its all-Negro units * * * There were no longer any all-Negro Marine units."

To most Americans that part of the Nichols story which is newsworthy will come as a heartening revelation. Couple it with the announcement from Tuskegee Institute that it has quit publishing the Lynch Letter because lynchings are no longer an index to race relations in the United States; the two together suggest that we may be doing much better than we know. Neither item is likely of publication in the Soviet press. But since the pivotal events of which Nichols writes occurred three years ago, and until now the nation has had only small bites of the story, there is room for remark that on the home front we are extravagantly wasteful of our own successes.

It is in the backward glance that Mr. Nichols, though ardent toward his subject and exceptionally sympathetic toward the services, fails somewhat of objectivity in relating why things did not move faster. There is insufficient recognition that the problem was vast indeed, that time itself had to provide part of the solution, and that the retarded pace was due less to mean prejudice within the military structure than to the mountainous social obstacles which lay without.

Because my name and role find mention in the book, some personal reflection should be pardonable. In minor capacities, I have had some experience with race problems within the services, first as commander of a Negro company in World War I, next as writer of the policy which formed the 442d (American-Japanese) Combat Team in World War II and, last, as an analyst of the integrated units in Korea. I would simply bear witness that I always found goodwill toward the object among my superiors and associates in the Army, and that where action was slowed it was because of reasonable doubt that a valid opportunity existed.

In calling the Army the mule of the service team prior to Korea, Nichols would seem to imply that it was least willing to undertake social reform. That discounts wholly the great difference between Army relationships with the people and those of other services. It is a much more sensitive body because of size and propinquity; its relative social inertia is inherent in its role.

In Korea success was made possible by failure. There was a critical shortage of white rifle replacements. Integration was mothered by necessity. Once it had proved good under ordeal by fire, all concerned rallied to the opportunity, though some were slower to see it than others. Had there not been abundant goodwill, the Far East Command would not have reformed its policy, nor could its example have inspired like action elsewhere.

True progress within a General Staff is possible only when a case can be made on the basis of superior data; then all doors swing open. But it is a truly felicitous thing that a nation can change its ways because of the deathless courage of a few mixed rifle squads in the nameless ridges north of Parallel 38.

E

The Negro Takes His Just Place in His Country's Armed Services

BREAKTHROUGH ON THE COLOR FRONT.
By Lee Nichols. 235 pp. New York: Random House. $3.50.

Reviewed by
ROY WILKINS

Soldiers taking time out to eat on the Korean front   United Press—Hank Egoshi

AT THE beginning of World War II Negro Americans in uniform were virtually pariahs in their native land and in its armed services. They were segregated into four all Negro army units (with predominantly white officers), barred from the Marine Corps and what was then the Air Corps, barred from the Navy except as stewards, segregated into a few National Guard units, confined to their own separate recreation facilities on military posts, humiliated, insulted and often attacked by civilians and police in off-post areas.

In World War I their combat units fought with the French, not the A.E.F., and practically every Army man who wrote memoirs or evaluations thereafter used a few chapters to lambast Negroes as fighting men and to give vent to his personal views on Negroes as human beings. No one took the trouble to try to understand the irony involved in black Americans fighting in a Jim Crow army to "make the world safe for democracy" or to "crush the Hitler master race doctrine." Negroes didn't feel good fighting for something they did not enjoy at home or even while they were fighting and dying. It is understandable, then, as a backward look is taken, that they might at times have fought indifferently.

Against this backdrop Lee Nichols has told how the Air Force, the Army, the Marines and finally the Navy have abandoned racial segregation and found to the amasement of all concerned that works (b) it produces fighting force and

The Air Force made the quickest and cleanest break with the past under its first Secretary of Air, Stuart Symington, now United States Senator from Missouri. With the backing of the late James V. Forrestal, Secretary of the Navy and later the first Secretary of Defense, Symington moved swiftly toward integration. After careful preparation the Air Force in 1949 issued a directive and within a matter of weeks the new policy was in effect. Today, along with the Marines, it has the most complete integration.

Under Forrestal the Navy had begun work on a policy of no discrimination and while thorough and sincere, it did not match the Air Force in performance or speed. However, progress has been steady and today only one problem remains to be solved: the disproportionate number of Negroes bunched in the Steward's branch.

The Army was much slower in moving to a new pattern. The author relates that Gen. Douglas MacArthur was cold to the idea of mixing troops in the Far East. Under Gen. Eisenhower Negro platoons were used alongside Whites in the dire emergency of the Battle of the Bulge, but neither Eisenhower nor the Pentagon would continue the experiment once the battle was won.

However, Korea forced integration. In battle so far from home it became difficult to replace Negroes with Negroes and Whites with Whites. Mixing became a military necessity. It worked beyond any one's dreams. Later integration was instituted in Europe, then in

training centers in America and finally was spread to practically all sections of the Army.

An important chapter details the damage dealt our foreign relations by American racial practices. Our men in uniform were our showcase abroad and the new armed services policy was an effective countermove that drew some of the teeth of the savage Soviet propaganda on mistreatment of Negroes.

Most astonishing and satisfying revelation in the changeover was the relative equanimity with which it was accepted by Southerners. Extensive sampling by Pentagon teams of social scientists came up with tradition-shattering statements by white Southern officers and enlisted men.

The impact on civilian life is yet to be measured, but the author cites the successful integration of schools on Army posts as a portent for desegregation of civilian schools. This veritable social revolution occurring, of all places, in the hard-bitten military establishment, could be, as the newspaperman-author suggests, one of the biggest stories of the twentieth century. For both the crusader and the skeptic this book, filled with the drama of official fact rather than exhortation and oratory, is a significant contribution to the continuing effort to build a dynamic and meaningful democracy in terms of human relations.

Roy Wilkins is Administrator of the National Association for the Advancement of Colored People.

F

RACES
The Unbunching

Mom, this is something I want you or Dad to do quick. They are mixing the niggers in the same barracks with us. If everyone's parents write their Congressmen to ask for something to be done about it, it will. Mom, please don't let me down. Quick!

Such anguished pleas were suddenly commonplace in June 1949, a month after the U.S. Air Force set out to abolish its all-Negro units. The integration of whites and Negroes, everyone agreed, would take many years, perhaps decades. Yet within a few months, the Air Force had broken through its color barrier. And by 1954, in the Army, Air Force, Navy and Marines, white and colored men worked together, marched together and learned to fight side by side. Not all of them liked it; but everyone accepted it.

Across the desk of Lee Nichols, a night rewrite man for the United Press in Washington, passed the terse Pentagon announcements and the brief press dispatches that were the communiqués in the war against armed-forces segregation—the Unknown War, as Nichols came to know it. Nichols became fascinated in the subject, and his interest led to previously secret files, to military bases, to scores of interviews. His book, *Breakthrough on the Color Front* (Random House; $3.50), published this week, is the most complete report to date on a war already in the mop-up stage.

The Bug-Out Song. Throughout U.S. history, Negroes have fought—and died —in the nation's wars (and Crispus Attucks, a runaway slave, was the first to fall in the Boston Massacre of 1770, prelude to the American Revolution). Yet always the verdict was the same: in combat, Negro units were "unreliable"—a euphemism for an uglier word. Even in the Korean war—nearly three years after President Truman's 1948 order for armed-forces equality—the classic story was of Negroes who fled from battle, then huddled around a campfire singing *The Bug Out Boogie*, the "official song of the (Negro) 24th Infantry Regiment":

When them Chinese mortars begins to thud,
The old Deuce-Four begins to bug . . .

But even as that tale went its round, segregation was ending—and with it the old belief in "bug out" as an inborn Negro weakness. The Navy, under the firm hand of James Forrestal, had started integration first of all, but soon began to run aground on service traditions. The Air

Force started its successful program less than a year after the Truman order, and the Marine Corps moved ahead. The Army, as Author Nichols says, was "the mule of the military team." Korea changed that; there simply were not enough white replacements, and field commanders were forced to fill in with Negroes. Once away from his Jim Crow unit, the Negro was a different soldier. How different became readily apparent in the results of Project Clear, an Army survey of the new racial policy. Items:

¶ On the test of standing up to mass attack, where Negro soldiers had had a reputation for taking to their heels, 85% of the officers interviewed in Korea said that Negroes in mixed units performed "about the same" as whites.

¶ In care of weapons, a phase of soldiering in which the Negro had been charged with laxity, 90% of the officers said "integrated" Negroes were on a par with whites.

INTEGRATED G.I.s IN KOREA
Why can't it be like that all over?

Nichols found only about 10,000 persons still serving in the Army's all-Negro units, with some 190,000 absorbed in regular outfits. The Air Force, with about 66,000 Negroes, has no segregated groups. Neither has the Marine Corps. Only the Navy trails in the wake: its stewards' branch (ships' servants) has one white

enlisted man and more than 11,000 Negroes, about 48% of the service's Negroes. Instead of breaking up the stewards' branch, the Navy is recruiting Filipinos to dilute the Negro concentration of the stewards, a solution that is not going to solve anything.

Even Chaplains & Psychiatrists. How does the policy of nonsegregation work in human terms? To find out, Nichols visited military and naval bases, most of them in the South. There are, he learned, virtually no race incidents at posts. Swimming pools, athletics, post exchanges, movies—and work—are shared (although Negroes are generally "discouraged" from attending white dances). At Camp Lejeune, N.C., Nichols saw a white Marine waiter approach a billiards-playing Negro sergeant and ask, in a respectful Southern drawl: "May I get you something, sir?" A Negro chaplain offhandedly told Nichols: "I'm just another chaplain; fellows come to see me regardless of race." A Negro Air Force psychiatrist said he had successfully treated several difficult mental cases involving the wives of white officers and men; it was a matter of routine. On the bases, the wives of Negroes and white men chatted casually over their clotheslines. An Army post commander described the situation simply: "There are no problems."

But there is a problem: the civilian world now lags far behind the military. Said an Army brigadier general: "What worries me is that a military career for a Negro is about the top he can get." A Negro G.I. said it in a different way: the Negro "begins to see the fellows getting along in the Army and begins to say to himself, it would be so goddam nice if it could be like that all over."

Although Jim Crow still applies in most Southern communities, even there the breakthrough is felt. Pentagon files tell of Southern restaurants being opened to Negro soldiers in uniform, and of white Southern families inviting Negro servicemen home to dinner or for a weekend. A significant then-*v.*-now example of the social change: on Aug. 13, 1906, Negro soldiers of the 25th Infantry Regiment rode into Brownsville, Texas, a hotbed of racial disorder, shooting into homes where people lay sleeping, killing a bartender, wounding a policeman. Brownsville did not forget quickly—but last year the First Presbyterian Church of Brownsville invited Negroes from a nearby air base to attend any or all of its services, right along with whites.

Early last year, an Army general saw the whole problem clearly. Said he of Negroes: "In civilian life, they are bunched. They've got to be unbunched." In 1954, the unbunching was well under way.

Color Line Vanishes in Services

By John G. Norris
Post Reporter

BIG news stories don't always break with a flash; sometimes they unveil so gradually you almost miss them. That's what has happened in a silent revolution which has taken place in the armed forces of the United States in the last few years.

This perhaps most conservative segment of our national life has performed a social aboutface and wiped out racial segregation. Acting under orders from the President and Commander in Chief, the services have just about completed the job.

Former President Truman's postwar directive on the subject was, of course, well known. So was the opposition to the move, within and without the services, and so were the forecasts that it would bring race trouble in the ranks and weaken American military power generally.

The news is that it works. If we are to believe the evidence set forth in a revealing new book, the new social pattern is working successfully at military bases both in the North and South, at home and overseas.

Not Merely Training

"BREAKTHROUGH on the Color Front," by United Press Reporter Lee Nichols (Random House, $3.50), gives eyewitness pictures of the situation at posts, interviews with men in the ranks and local commanders and quotations from official reports to show that nonsegregation is now accepted throughout the services.

He also makes a good case, bolstered by quotes from officers and from an Army survey in Korea, that it has strengthened rather than weakened the United States militarily.

Reporting on visits to many bases in the South, Nichols says:

"Negroes and whites in the armed forces were not just training and fighting together; they were eating at the same tables, sleeping next to one another and drinking beer together at military post canteens. They were going to church and the movies together, often attending the same dances.

"Families of white and Negro servicemen were coming more and more to live next to one another on military reservations. Their wives gossiped over the clothesline and learned to be friendly neighbors. Their children attended schools together on military posts."

NICHOLS says that swimming pools as well as athletics, post canteens and movies at Fort Jackson, S. C., and other Southern bases are completely shared. Two service clubs often are maintained, one largely white and the other largely Negro, but both races are admitted to both clubs.

Mixed dances are "discouraged" or even prohibited at some Southern bases, but mingling of Negro and white couples at canteens and soda fountains was reported by Nichols.

The 234-page book traces the history of the Negro in the armed forces, showing that segregation was the pattern until the latter days of World War II. The Navy, under the late Secretary James Forrestal, was the first to establish racial integration. It works satisfactorily, but half of the Navy's 23,000 Negroes are messmen and still are segregated in fact.

The Air Force integrated next. It succeeded, says Nichols, because Air Secretary Stuart Symington called in his generals and told them to "stop the double talk and act." There were a few crackdowns, and then the order was accepted. Today, the 66,000 USAF Negroes are completely integrated.

Army chiefs, however, protested that the military services should not be "an instrument of social evolution" and strongly resisted the President's policy. Not until Korea did segregation start to become a fact.

Speeded Up Training

CURIOUSLY, the first big break in segregation came at Fort Jackson, S. C. Faced with a heavy influx of recruits and mounting demands from the front, Brig. Gen. Frank McConnell, the commander, tried integration on his own initiative to speed up training. It worked.

In Korea, some division commanders started integrating their units and reported that the men fought well. But Gen. Douglas MacArthur's headquarters stopped the experiment, Nichols reports. Later, under Gen. Mathew B. Ridgway, all-Negro units were broken up. After the resulting mixed units had been fighting for some time, interview teams were sent out to question battalion and company commanders.

"Of 185 officers who completed the forms," Nichols reports, "majorities of 66 to 90 percent rated Negroes in mixed units 'about on a par' with white soldiers on nearly every one of 28 aspects of combat behavior.

"On the crucial test of standing up to mass attack, where Negro soldiers in the past had sometimes broken and run, 85 percent of the officers found that Negroes in mixed units performed 'about the same' as white soldiers."

Rated by Buddies

THE survey teams also questioned 1563 white and 221 Negro soldiers in integrated infantry squads scattered through four divisions. The white soldiers reported they had observed "slightly more instances of good morale, courage and judgment" among whites than Negroes; about the same number of instances of lack of courage and poor judgment, and slightly fewer specific cases of poor morale among Negroes.

The never released survey, said Nichols, found that 11 to 15 percent of the men who had served in integrated units rated mixed units superior in morale to all-white units. The explanation offered for this feeling and for the great improvement among Negro soldiers assigned to integrated units: The Negro gains pride and self-respect and both whites and Negroes are "put on their mettle."

Today, less than 10,000 of the Army's 200,000 Negroes are in segregated units and all, say Pentagon chiefs, will be integrated by this summer.

Next on the list of integration advocates, he adds, is "upgrading" of the Pentagon's Negro civilian workers, who are almost entirely in the low-pay brackets; ending of segregation in the National Guard, and breaking up of the solidly Negro messmen's branch of the Navy.

The success of integration in the armed forces, the author believes, has brought these important results:

1. It has blunted Russia's best propaganda weapon among the colored populations of the world.

2. It has increased our military power and potential by more efficient use of our manpower. Army leaders generally were right, Nichols concludes, in branding all-Negro combat units "unreliable." The evidence from Korea, he says, is that integrated fighting units there were largely on a par with all-white units.

3. It has hastened the abolition of segregation in civilian life: by example; by changing race attitudes of youths leaving the services, and by its influence on communities near military posts.

H

Col B.O. Davis Jr
Hq 51st Ftr Intcp Wg
APO 60 care PM
San Francisco

Friday 2 April

Dear Lee,

I received the copy of "Breakthrough"
today and have just finished reading it. I
found it very accurate as I compared it
with my memory of a good many of
the things you mention, and also very
readable. All in all, I enjoyed it very
much, and I think it will go a long
way to increase the understanding of
those who know less about the subject
than you and I know.

I'm sorry you didn't autograph
the book, but maybe I'll get you to do
that some time in the future. I appreciate
very much your mailing it to me.

Sincerely,
B.

I

A Civil Rights Victory

Reviewed by JOSEPH B. ROBISON

BREAKTHROUGH ON THE COLOR FRONT. By Lee Nichols. Random House. 235 pp. $3.50

Ten years ago, millions of American men were being subjected by their government to a prolonged and effective course in racism. Placed in a segregated Army and forced to conform to its customs, the prejudices of those who were white were strengthened and the tendencies towards self-hate of those who were Negroes were accelerated. Five years ago, the situation was much the same, but a revolution had started. Today that revolution is virtually complete.

The story is told in *Breakthrough on the Color Front.* The author ends his story with a remark made by Brig. Gen. Lloyd Hopwood, deputy chief of Air Force personnel, as he stopped one day to talk with the author. Nichols was looking over letters from Air Force commanders describing the success of the integration program. "I like to look through them myself once in a while," Hopwood said. "It kind of restores my faith in human nature." Any reader of this book must have the same reaction.

Mr. Nichols, a United Press reporter and rewrite man, spent his spare time for more than a year acquiring his facts. He has reported them clearly and soberly. He presents both the good and the bad aspects, though he tends to hasten somewhat over the latter. He makes it plain that there is still opposition to the desegregation policy in the armed forces, in Congress and among civilians, but that it is far too weak to have any effect.

A good deal of the information is of the "now-it-can-be-told" variety: how President Truman's Executive Order of 1948 against discrimination, which did not mention segregation, was interpreted by individual commands, some as meaning nothing, others as meaning more than anyone seems to have intended. How the Army brass deliberately misled the Fahy Committee, established to police that Order, by pretending they were ending segregation when they were not, only to be double-crossed by lower echelon officers who ended segregation in their commands and used the Order as justification. Most striking was the repeal of the statutes enacted in the 1860's specifi-

Feb. 4, 1954

Dear Lee :

Thanks for the copy of "Breakthrough on the Color Front" and for the over-generous inscription in it. I have read it through , and I congratulate you on it. You have done a splendid job of gathering the material,putting it in order and of writing it. The result is that you have a very good book and an important one. In it you have the authentic evidence of one of the most important social advances of our time, and for a thousand years and more the historians and the scholars must go to it ~~in~~ for the facts. It makes good reading too. I hope it will sell as well as it deserves,both that it may have large influence and ~~that~~ *it may* ~~to~~ bring some money to the Nichols family. I hope Random House , either now or later, will get out a cheaper paper cover edition, something to sell for a dollar or less so that the Negroes can buy it. They should treasure it next to the Bible.

Why don't you and Neil make another visit to Southampton -- say in the Spring when the weather is better? We should like to have you come again and talk things over.

The best of luck

Mr. Lee Nichols,

Washington, D.C?.

Neil MacNeil

From former editor of *New York Times*. He was the motivating force that led Nichols to write the book.

K

NiemanReports

April, 1954

Army Fires Jim Crow

by Charles Eberhardt

BREAKTHROUGH ON THE COLOR
FRONT. By Lee Nichols. Random
House, New York. $3.50.

Jim Crow has been discharged from
the armed forces of the United States,
and an alert newsman has dug out the
story to make a thorough, straightforward,
and very hopeful book.

Lee Nichols, a rewriteman on the night
desk in the Washington bureau of the
United Press Associations, recognized the
profound implications of a casual Pentagon press release. He developed that
hint into this story of the end of racial
segregation in the military services. He
thinks defense department "integration"
may turn out to be one of the biggest
stories of this century, and his book makes
a good case for that judgment.

To find out how far integration has
gone, and how it is working, Nichols
traveled to bases in both North and South;
he talked to Pentagon officials; and studied
reports of social scientists who were assigned to keep a watchful, professional
eye on the transition. He interviewed
combat veterans and new recruits, three
star generals and buck privates, Pentagon
wheels and Negro sailors. To his report
of their responses he adds a brief historical survey of the role of the Negro in the
military forces of the U.S., a role as old
as the nation.

The swift changes since 1949 followed
a limited beginning during World War II
when the Negro breached the color front
to win the right to attend non-segregated
officers candidates schools and then won
admission to pilot training.

That beach head was expanded until
today it includes virtually every kind of
duty in all services, the field of civilian
employment at military bases, and the
schools provided for children of servicemen.

How are these innovations working?
After weighing the evidence, Nichols
concludes that the immediate consequences
are improved efficiency and morale among
all service personnel, regardless of color.
The ultimate consequences could be that
"biggest story of the century."

The evidence came from professional
soldiers who've seen integration working,
even at Biloxi, Miss. Many of them saw
the first, and critical, experiment when, in
Korea, the pressing necessity of battle
forced integration of troops on the line.
Korea, as Nichols puts it, converted
the army.

That conversion had repercussions
everywhere. It provided clinching answers to the military commanders who
were prone to drag their feet to delay
the change that Truman and then Eisenhower had made federal policy. And
the Korea conversion evoked a strange
silence from Congress; even legislators
from the deep South hesitated to attack
an accomplished fact.

Opposition to using Negroes in integrated units hadn't been without basis. Nichols describes official reports of poor per-
formances of segregated Negro troops
in Korea, in World War II, and in World
War I. In doing this he performs a
service by putting into proper perspective
rumors that grew from vague accounts
of Negro outfits that faded away when
the shooting began.

The author treats this touchy issue, and
others like the explosive question of military policy toward the relationships of
men and women of different races—with
calm and competence.

This is objective reporting as it should
be: factual, comprehensive, and balanced;
by no means superficial. Only a bigot could
read this account of a courageous and
successful experiment without feeling
grateful to Nichols for putting it down
plainly and dispassionately.

From DEMOCRATIC DIGEST, July 1954

Korean Heroes Prove That

ALL AMERICANS CAN FIGHT

By Lee Nichols

Condensed from Breakthrough On The Color Front

On December 5, 1950, a squadron of U. S. Navy planes from the aircraft carrier U.S.S. Leyte, off Korea, was bombing and strafing Chinese Communist troops in the battle of the Chosin Reservoir.

One of the Navy planes was hit and went down. Crash-landing in a rough field five miles in front of the American lines, it burst into flames.

The pilot of a companion plane, spotting the burning craft, landed nearby and ran to the rescue. Unable to open the canopy to get the pilot out, he packed the fuselage with snow to keep the fire back. A Marine helicopter landed with axes and rescue equipment, but was too late to save the flier, who died in the pyre of his plane.

The pilot who died was Ens. Jesse L. Brown, officially listed as the first Negro pilot in Navy history. The man who risked death or capture to save him was Lt. (j.g.) Thomas J. Hudner, a white pilot, who was awarded the Medal of Honor for his heroism.

On June 2, 1951, a platoon officer of Company C, 24th Infantry Regiment, 24th U. S. Division, was wounded during an attack on a Communist-held hill near Chopo-ri, Korea. A 21-year-old sergeant assumed command of the platoon, led a handful of men up a steep hill and personally wiped out two enemy positions with grena⌐ rifle fire, killing six enem

Devastating enemy ⌐ ing from hea····

M

Segregation In Army Virtually Abolished

By LEE NICHOLS
United Press Correspondent

WASHINGTON, July 5.—The Army virtually has completed its program of ending segregation of its white and Negro soldiers, an Army spokesman said today.

He said more than 98 per cent of Army Negroes now are "integrated" into white units and that "no more than 15" all-Negro units remain, none larger than a company.

'Specialized' Units Remain

Those Negro units still in existence are largely "specialized" units. They are being de-segregated by attrition—the normal process of discharge and assignment. As a result, it is taking a little longer to integrate them, the spokesman said.

But military racial experts said that to all intents and purposes the Army is now "integrated."

This is a historic step, completing the basic integration of the armed forces begun in 1945, when the Navy tried the "bold" experiment of mixing Negroes in with white crews of 25 auxiliary ships — tankers, patrol craft *and the like.*

All Navy Berths Open

In 1946 the late Navy Secretary James Forrestal ordered all berths in the Navy opened to Negroes, and barred separation of sleeping or eating facilities.

In 1949, the Air Force ordered segragation ended throughout its world-wide command.

The Army, which took small steps toward integration starting with unsegragated training of officers—at the start of the Second World War, began a real breakdown of its color lines after the start of the Korean war four years ago.

N

February 18, 1954

Dear Mr. Nichols:

Thank you very much for your letter of
February 6, 1954, telling me of the publication of
your book, BREAKTHROUGH ON THE COLOR FRONT.

I have just come from Columbus, Ohio, and
saw a copy of your book which Mr. P. L. Prattis of
"The Pittsburgh Courier" had. He told me what an
excellent job you have done and suggested that I read
it. Since that time, I have seen some reviews which
also have whetted my appetite.

I hope the book will have wide circulation
and I am sure it will have great influence for good.
It tells a story which needs to be told now that the
trend is definitely in the direction of integration.
It will help to persuade some of the doubters that
this thing can be done.

Sincerely yours,

CAMPBELL C. JOHNSON
Colonel, Infantry

Mr. Lee Nichols
United Press Associations
National Press Building
Washington 4, D. C.

O

1944: 100th Fighter Squadron. Left to Right: Then Capt. Benjamin O. Davis, Jr. with Capt. Richard Caesar, Engineering Officer, Flight Crew Member Ground, Col. Felix Vidal, 306th Wing, Deputy Commander.

P

Left: Col. Benjamin O. Davis, Jr. Right: Capt. Andrew Turner, Cmdr. of 100th Fighter Squadron.

Q

Center: Gen. Benjamin O. Davis, Jr., with Visitor Staff Sgt. Joe Louis and Other Members of 332 Fighter Group, Ramitelli, Italy, 1944 or 1945.

R

Lt. Gen. Benjamin O. Davis, Jr. Awarding Legion of Merit to Maj. Kenneth Dempster.

Brigadier Gen. Benjamin O. Davis, Sr., 1st African-American General.

T

Photograph of President Bill Clinton with Lee Aspin, Secretary of Defense, and General Colin L. Powell, Chief of Staff.

U

Appendix A

Response of the Director of the Defense Equal Opportunity Management Institute (DEOMI) to the Author's Questionnaire

Q. and A. with Col. Ronald M. Joe (Patrick Air Force Base, Florida)

Q: What is the purpose of DEOMI?

A: To enhance readiness of the armed forces through assisting commanders to ensure fairness and equal opportunity among military personnel; to train, educate and conduct research in the area of equal opportunity, cultural diversity and fairness; and to train equal opportunity staff advisers for all the services, active and reserve, including the Coast Guard.

Q: What has DEOMI accomplished so far?

A: It has trained over 12,000 service members at the Institute and provided mobile training for thousands more. DEOMI sends mobile training teams to military bases throughout the world. The impact has been improved readiness of the armed services and assistance in achieving equal opportunity. It has influenced military thinking and policy concerning the commitment to equal opportunity and fairness.

Q: Has the military, and its policy and efforts to improve equal opportunity, had any impact on civilian society?

A: Integration in the military has set the standards for and made easier integration in civilian society. People outside the military work on military bases and there is spin-off from the equal opportunity mandates and practices on the bases. People on bases live outside the bases without regard to race and this influences the local communities. It is extremely important to understand that the training we give to military people in the field of equal opportunity is unequaled in civilian society. We concentrate on behavior and also on education. Our children are an important element in this. Our children carry over their enlightenment to civilian children. They are well travelled. My son at age 18 had travelled 12 years in Europe. He did not concentrate on racial differences. Ethnicity has no value for him when choosing friends or associates. Our kids bring that perspective to the communities in which they live.

Q: Has DEOMI expanded its equal opportunity training beyond the U.S. military?

A: We offer regular training on a space available basis to communities and corporations throughout the U.S. Some local police departments ask for training. I went to Los Angeles to consult with the Los Angeles police department, and also consulted with the Washington, D.C., police department. We also consulted with local school boards. We have provided speakers and discussion leaders to some of the major 500 corporations. Currently we are having meetings with representatives of the Russian military establishment to share our experience with dealing with ethnic minorities. Our goal is to share with them the U.S. experience in equal opportunity and cultural diversity; to tell them what we do, assess their needs. In the spring of 1993 I visited Russia and met with officials of the military. They do have ethnic problems, and problems connected with their "humanization" program. We expect five to six Russian officers to attend DEOMI's 16-week course in 1994. We are sending some or our people to Warsaw, Poland, to work with former Warsaw Pact personnel. We are offering representatives of the former Soviet bloc our experience in promoting equal opportunity and cultural diversity.

Q: Is the U.S. military a leader in promoting equal opportunity?

A: The Defense Department (military and civilian) is clearly a leader. There is still a lot do. We have to continue to work on all issues: race, sexism, religious intolerance, sex discrimination and opportunities for women. There has been a lot of progress but we must continue across the entire range to work at constant improvement to make sure our forces are ready from a human relations and human readiness standpoint.

Q: The Defense Department Equal Opportunity Office reports that there is over-representation of blacks in the military justice system, notably in courts-martial. Is DEOMI doing anything about this?

A: We are studying it to try to find out the cause and what we can do about it. This same phenomenon exists in our society at large, but worse. As a result of our research, we hope we can provide information to the society at large. It may take a while.

Appendix B

Gays, Blacks and the Military

A memorandum prepared by Adam Yarmolinsky,
Regents Professor of Public Policy in the University of
Maryland system. Prof. Yarmolinsky was formerly
Special Assistant to then-Secretary of Defense Robert
McNamara.

Some light might be shed on the issue of gays in the military by recalling the work of two presidential commissions that looked into the integration of the military going back over 40 years. The Fahy Committee, appointed by President Truman and headed by the late Judge Charles Fahy, found that the Navy and Air Force were generally moving satisfactorily to carry out Truman's Executive Order of July 26, 1948, providing for "equality of treatment and opportunity for all persons in the armed services. . . ." The Fahy Committee, however, found the Army dragging its feet and took steps that helped move the Army to eventual abolition of segregation.

Another parallel with the black experience in the military goes back over 30 years ago when President Kennedy created a second committee, the Gesell Committee on Equal Opportunity in the Armed Forces. That committee was asked to deal particularly with discrimination against military men and women and their dependents in civilian communities around military bases. There may be lessons in this second round in the civil rights battle within the military.

Early in the Kennedy administration it became clear that there were continuing problems in the treatment of blacks in the military and very serious problems outside the base gates, particularly in the South. There were reports of married black officers and non-coms who couldn't find landlords willing to rent to them within 50 miles of the base, and having to settle for converted chicken coops an hour's drive or more away from their work. Many reports told of local bars and restaurants which blacks could not enter, even of local police stopping mixed groups walking out of base gates together and telling them to "break it up."

Early in the Kennedy administration, Deputy Secretary of Defense Gilpatric issued a directive to the three service secretaries telling them to remove remaining vestiges of discrimination and to deal with off-base discrimination. The directive got side-tracked in the military bureaucracy and nothing happened.

I was then the Special Assistant to Secretary of Defense Robert McNamara. I recalled the work of the Fahy Committee and its impetus in pushing military integration to completion at a time when the prevailing view, chiefly in the Army, was that integration would impair military efficiency. Another committee of outsiders, I thought, might take a fresh look at off-base discrimination and propose solutions which could not be ignored.

McNamara and Gilpatric responded enthusiastically. We found a worthy successor to Judge Fahy in Gerhard Gesell (who died recently after more than 25 years as a distinguished federal judge). He was then a Washington lawyer in private practice. We made up a list of other members, all prominent civilians, black and white.

After an extensive investigation, including on-the-scene visits to military bases at home and overseas, the committee's key recommendation was that off-base establishments that discriminated against any service personnel should be placed off limits to all service personnel. A bar that would not serve black soldiers would lose all its service patronage. A landlord who would not rent to blacks could not rent to any service families.

Publication of the Gesell report, I believe, made initiation of the "off-limits" policy inevitable. A directive from the Secretary's office set up a special office to monitor the new program. We brought in to direct it Alfred Fitt, whom I had met in 1958 when he was counsel to Mennen G. "Soapy" Williams, then governor of Michigan. Fitt, who died last fall, later went on to a distinguished career as counsel for the Congressional Budget Office.

Fitt's first assignment was to draft a new directive. I took the draft to McNamara who made a few changes to soften the language a bit and signed it. A copy of the marked-up draft somehow found its way to Louisiana Congressman Eddie Hebert, an unreconstructed segregationist, who immediately assumed that the first draft was my work, and, in a speech on the House floor, denounced my "satanic passion for integration" which, he claimed, waving a copy of the marked-up draft, had been too extreme even for McNamara.

Fitt visited Southern bases to uncover problems and work out solutions. His first report, from Mobile, Alabama, told us that of all the Gulf Coast beaches within reasonable distance from military bases, there was none where a black man or woman could swim. Fitt's diplomatic skill began to produce results. That he had the authority of the Secretary of Defense behind him as well made a difference. So did the provisions of the new directive making elimination of discrimination an element in the efficiency rating of base commanders.

In 1967, almost a year after I left the Pentagon, the off-limits authority in the directive was employed to desegregate off-base housing, initially in a community in Southern Maryland. In a Twentieth Century Fund study, entitled *The Military Establishment: Its Impact on American Society*, published in 1971, I stated that, "Restaurants, bars, taxi services, even bathing beaches near military bases were desegregated after military intervention, usually brought about by complaints of Negro servicemen."

With or without the stimulus of a Gesell Committee, one hopes that gay rights will be more promptly vindicated.

APPENDIX C

Present Situation of African Americans in the U.S. military (June, 1993)

It has not been possible, in the time available to me, to give a full and authentic accounting of the current status of non-discrimination and the situation of African Americans in the U.S. armed forces. This summary relies on official Department of Defense policy documents and statements of responsible military authorities; and the comments and findings of some of the military's principal outside observers and critics—such as the National Association for the Advancement of Colored People, the chairman of the U.S. Civil Rights Commission and others.

To begin with, it appears that the U.S. military establishment is probably the most advanced, in terms of anti-discriminatory regulations and practices, of any major American institution. This was true when my book was written in 1953; and it is equally true today.

Les Aspin, Secretary of Defense under President Clinton, when chairman of the House Armed Services Committee said at a public hearing of the Defense Policy Panel of that committee on July 29, 1992, that, "Today, the military is one of, if not the, most thoroughly integrated institution in American society."

Dr. Edwin Dorn, Assistant Secretary of Defense for Personnel and Readiness under President Clinton, then a senior staff member of the Brookings Institution in Washington, D.C., said in a statement to the House Armed Services Committee on March 4, 1991:

"The military was the first major American institution to adopt and implement equal opportunity. Many of our civilian institutions have been slow to make such a commitment, and the results show in their work forces, especially at the managerial and executive levels. The Army had black officers commanding white soldiers in combat years before some of our universities entrusted black professors with the responsibility of teaching white undergraduates. It was not surprising that the Joint Chiefs of Staff had a black chairman [Gen. Colin Powell] before any Fortune 500 company had a black chief executive."

Even the NAACP, while reporting an increase in allegations of discrimination by black military personnel in Germany in late 1992, stated in a report by James D. Williams, director of NAACP public relations, in the NAACP magazine *Crisis* of March, 1993, that, "What was clear, even before the hearings and briefings began [in military bases in Europe], was that compared to other institutions, the military is miles ahead of them all in providing equal opportunity for African-Americans and other minorities. You did not need the statistics to show this. All it required was a look around on any of the installations to see the stripes on the sleeves and the bars, eagles and stars on the shoulders, and to note who was giving the orders, to make this abundantly clear."

There have been recent charges of racial discrimination in a number of military services, notably by the NAACP and by Dr. Arthur Fletcher, chairman of the U.S. Civil Rights Commission—charges that will be summarized later. But it is worthy of note that Milton D. Morris, Vice President for Research of the leading black "think tank," the Joint Center for Political and Economic Studies, told this author in June of this year that, "The Army has outperformed the rest of society in terms of equal opportunity." He acknowledged there were substantial numbers of claims of discrimination "in individual cases" but added, "I don't see major institutional criticism or complaints. I see particular problems, tied to specific locations. By and large I don't see any systematic racial problems."

And a Congressional staff source, who monitors the situation of blacks in the military, told this author that, "The United States military is one of the most integrated institutions in America today. There are no restrictions on recruiting, training, duty, combat, or use of facilities by blacks." This source also acknowledged there are cases of friction among African Americans and whites in the military establishment sufficient to be reported to the Pentagon, but said he "would not put them in the serious category."

"The military establishment is probably the most integrated segment of U.S. society and has made tremendous progress towards equal opportunity," this Congressional source added.

The Defense Department (DoD) policy on non-discrimina-

226

tion, officially known as "Equal Opportunity," is clear and un-
equivocal. DoD Directive 1350.2 of Nov. 23, 1988, currently in
force, states that it is DoD policy to "support the military EO
program as an integral element in total force readiness...and enforce at all levels of activity the EO provisions of this Directive to
developing operating EO policies and programs."

It declares it to be DoD policy to "ensure the Military Services
(to include the Reserve components) maintain military EO and
affirmative action programs." It then states:

"Discrimination that adversely affects persons or groups based
on race, color, religion, gender, age, or national origin, and that
is not supported legally, is contrary to good order and discipline,
and is counterproductive to combat readiness and mission accomplishment. Discrimination of this nature shall not be con-
doned or tolerated."*

The policy directive calls for "education and training in EO
and human relations at installations and fleet unit commands,
Military Accession points, and throughout the professional military education...system, as part of the overall effort to achieve
equal opportunity."

It states it to be DoD policy to "ensure that all on-base activities and, to the extent of the ability of DoD, any off-base activities available to military personnel are open to all military personnel and their authorized family members regardless of race, color,
religion, age, physical or mental handicap, gender, or national
origin...."

*This provision exempts the requirement, both legal and by regulation,
that women be excluded from certain combat roles, a requirement currently under revision; and legal requirements as to age, certain physical
requirements such as weight, etc.

The directive declares it to be DoD policy to "oppose discrimination in off-base housing directed against military personnel and their authorized family members. Each commander shall take actions to overcome such discrimination and to impose off-limits sanctions in housing cases [where discrimination is proven]...."

Also stated is the policy to "Impose, as required, the off-limits sanction...in cases of discrimination involving places of public accommodations outside military establishments."

A significant aspect of the military's non-discrimination policy is a further requirement that commanders at all levels are to be judged, in their efficiency ratings, on their support of the Equal Opportunity directive. Also significant is the fact that EO training is given at all levels of the military establishment "including command-selectees and flag and general officers...."

According to a spokesman in the DoD Equal Opportunity Office, some form of EO training is given to all members of the military establishment. In basic training there is an introduction to EO policy on non-discrimination and sexual harassment. When a recruit enters the non-commissioned officer ranks, there are more detailed classes. Commanding officers are required to take a wider range of classes.

In the Army, for example, there are full-time "advisers" on equal opportunity at the brigade level and above (a brigade contains a minimum of 1,280 persons and is usually much larger). These "advisers"—enlisted men including corporals and sergeants but not commissioned officers* —are required to take 16 weeks of EO training at the Defense Equal Opportunity Management Institute (DEOMI), located at Patrick Air Force Base in

*At higher than brigade levels the EO advisers may be commissioned officers.

Florida. The major bloc of classes at DEOMI is in socialization; individual and group behavior; race, ethnic studies and intergroup relations; aspects of discrimination; EO staff adviser skills; and for the individual military services specific sections of instruction on the rules and regulations and policies of their respective services. The classes include courses on how to be an instructor in EO, how to deliver briefings, etc.

Below the brigade level, Army units have part-time EO advisers who are trained by the full-time DEOMI-trained EO advisers.

The Navy operated by "commands." There are EO advisers on major ships such as aircraft carriers and on large shore installations.

In the Air Force, EO is in the hands of "social action personnel" in a program that combines EO with drug and alcohol prevention.

The words "segregation" and "integration" are seldom used today in official military documents or statements. According to the DoD Equal Opportunity Office, the last all-black unit in the military was terminated in 1954 (see Appendix D). (The author has not been able, in the time available, to document the details of this action.)

It has also not been possible to learn exactly when segregation ended in the Navy's Stewards Branch. When this book was written in 1953 the Stewards Branch, which handled mess and quarters services for officers on ships and shore installations, was almost totally if not totally composed of black and Filipino sailors. In 1975 the Stewards Branch was merged with the Commissary rating in a new Mess Management Specialty rating. At the time of this writing, the Mess Management Specialists were composed of 15,898 personnel, including 47.7 percent "minorities." A breakdown by a Navy official showed a total of 7,544 whites,

5,130 blacks, 1,837 Filipinos, 934 Hispanics and presumably a smaller number of other minorities such as Asian and Native Americans.

It was stated by the Navy's EO office that there is no segregation of Mess Management personnel by race in sleeping, messing or other accommodations on ship or shore installations. The only exception is that females have separate berthing and toilet facilities. The Navy EO office says there is no special effort to recruit either blacks, Filipinos or other minorities for the Mess Management rating, nor is there any effort to assign blacks or other minorities to that rating once they are enlisted in the Navy. In fact, according to Navy EO officials, because of the concentration of minorities in certain branches of the Navy there is a "push" to get minorities into the underutilized ratings such as technical areas.

The current armed forces, as of June, 1993, consisted of 1,769,424 personnel, of which 346,347 or 19.6 percent were black.* The figures break down to 28 percent blacks in the Army; 16.1 percent in the Navy; 14.7 percent in the Air Force; and 17 percent in the Marines. These numbers are higher than the percentage of blacks in the U.S. population as a whole—slightly over 12 percent at latest census count. There will be discussion of the disproportion later.

At the officer level, the total number of black commissioned officers, from lieutenants through admirals and generals, in the military services was 17,305 or 6.9 percent. Warrant officers,

*Since my original book dealt exclusively with the issue of blacks in the military, I am not attempting to discuss the question of other minorities in this edition except where some of them crop up in quotations that I use.

between commissioned officers and enlisted men, were 1,942 black or 9.7 percent. The distribution of black generals and admirals in the services as of June, 1993, was as follows:

Army - 26, or 7.1 percent of all generals. The Army had one full general, Colin Powell, chairman of the Joint Chiefs of Staff, and 25 other generals of lower rank. General Powell's full general ship was listed as being 9.1 percent of all Army full generals.

Navy - 3 admirals of various levels, or 1.3 percent of all Navy admirals.

Air Force - 5 generals, or 1.7 percent of total Air Force generals.

Marines - 1 general, amounting to 1.5 percent of Marine generals.

The total black enlisted men and women in all the services comprised 327,100 or 21.8 percent to the total of 1,500,343 enlisted personnel.

Dr. Edwin Dorn, in his testimony to the House Armed Services Committee in 1991, said the Committee "may wish to ask whether the services are doing as much as they might to enhance the representation of blacks and other minorities in the officer corps. Some of the services are not doing at all well on this front. The Air Force, for example, experienced a decline in black officer accession during the 1980s." Dr. Dorn suggested a number of possible remedies for the low proportion of black officers in the military. As Assistant Secretary of Defense for Personnel and Readiness, with jurisdiction over the military EO program, he will be in a position to address this situation.

Of the disproportionate percentage of blacks in the military services overall, Dr. Dorn said that, "More often than not, complaints about the social makeup of the military are not really about the military. Rather they are about the inequities in the larger society." He said it was unfair to characterize "today's current enlistees as 'economic conscripts,' as young people forced to choose between destitution on the streets of our inner cities and combat danger in some distant land. Considering the civilian employment options that are available to high school graduates—generally low-wage service sector jobs with little long-term career potential—military service is a rational economic choice."

Dr. Dorn said that over the past several years he had interviewed hundreds of soldiers, from recruits in their first months of training to NCO's in the 82nd Airborne at Fort Bragg, North Carolina, and armored cavalry troops in Germany and that, "Generally, these men and women seemed to care less about their origins than about their destinations. They saw the military as a source of great opportunity, and themselves as professionals trained to fulfill an important responsibility. They did not see themselves as victims. We do them a disservice if we suggest they had no choice but to join the military."

Gen. Colin Powell, in an address to the NAACP annual convention in Houston, Texas, on July 11, 1991, said he had "never apologized to anybody when we're accused of having a disproportionate number of minorities who seek military careers. I am proud that we offer these kinds of opportunities." He said he belonged to "a profession which allowed me to progress according to my ability and to my dreams. The armed forces, we believe, come closer to the dream than any other institution in our society. We make it happen. We have allowed men and women of color to go as far as their talents take them. Many see the armed forces as a way up, as an opportunity."

The House Armed Services Subcommittee on Military Personnel and Compensation, in conjunction with the committee's

Defense Panel, issued a report on Sept. 14, 1992, that spoke of three phases in the "pattern of change" regarding race relations in the military:

Phase One - the move toward desegregation of the armed forces, centered on President Truman's Executive Order of July, 1948, calling for "equality of treatment and opportunity" in the armed forces. The report said the executive order "resulted in little real desegregation." (I do not regard this statement as accurate. See my chapters 9 and 10.)

Phase Two - the Korean War which built "momentum to integrate...when black soldiers pressed to be allowed to participate fully in the war effort. In addition, battlefield casualties needed to be replaced."

Phase Three - "The combination of pressure and necessity spurred the military leaders to make genuine change. This phase of the pattern saw the end of institutional segregation. The remaining combat restrictions for blacks were dropped. Blacks were assigned to all units and performed their missions with distinction."

The report reviewed some of the events which led to reports of racial difficulties during the Vietnam War. "By the mid-60s," it said, "the war in Vietnam was escalating, and race relations in the services became increasingly troubled. Black servicemen were being sent to Vietnam in numbers disproportionate to their number in the population as a whole. They also accounted for an equally disproportionate percentage of combat casualties [see below]. This situation fostered lingering resentment among black members of the military leading to heightened racial tensions....

"By 1970, racial conflict was beginning to hinder the war effort in Vietnam as incidents occurred on military installations both at home and abroad. In 1971, 40 black soldiers marched on the commanding general's headquarters at Chu Lai, Vietnam demanding an end to discrimination."

The report said that, "The watershed event that seriously focused the military on improving race relations took place in 1972. High profile racial incidents occurred on board the Navy aircraft carriers U.S.S. Kitty Hawk and U.S.S. Constellation...."

"The combination of dangers," the report continued, "finally forced the whole military to make a sustained, serious effort to stop racial discrimination." It described as one example steps taken by the Navy which included training of a cadre of race relations specialists and "mandatory racial awareness training for all levels of naval personnel." (Details of the services' current EO training programs were described earlier.)

During the Vietnam War there were many reports that blacks were suffering a higher rate of casualties than whites in battle. Dr. Dorn said that in 1965 and 1966, blacks made up 20 percent of the Army's battle deaths and 16 percent of all U.S. combat casualties in Southeast Asia. He added, however, that changes in Selective Service rules that led to the drafting of large numbers of white college students "evened out the combat risks in the end" and that "blacks made up about 12 percent of all U.S. military personnel who were killed in battle during the Vietnam conflict."

A more serious disproportion of black deaths was a potentiality in the Desert Storm War in 1991, according to Dorn. He said that roughly 25 percent of the U.S. Desert Storm contingent was black, "so if the coalition forces had become bogged down in a long ground war with Iraq, about one-fourth of the U.S. casualties would have been black. Since blacks were only one-eight of the nation's population, this level of combat exposure would be disproportionate, and grounds for resentment." However the Desert Storm operation was quickly successful and there have been no reported complaints about the level of black deaths in that war.

According to the Defense Department publication *Population Representation in the Military Services (fiscal year 1991, October 1992)*, the House Armed Services Committee, according to its then-chairman Les Aspin, "'spent some considerable time on this [the notion that blacks would bear a disproportionate share of fighting and dying in future wars] and came to a rather surprising conclusion about it. It's not true.'"*

To balance my summary of the current situation of blacks in the U.S. military, I consulted four sources outside the military establishment who monitor or have special concerns about the military racial situation: the National Association for the Advancement of Colored People (NAACP); the chairman of the U.S. Civil Rights Commission; the Vice President for Research of the Center for Political and Economic Studies, the leading "think tank" promoting the cause of blacks in American society; and a "Congressional staff source" with oversight responsibility for blacks in the military, who asked not to be further identified.

The NAACP, as noted earlier, reported a "major increase in the number of allegations of discrimination" received by its Eu-

---

*An informed source said it was believed that Aspin was relating the potential of black deaths to the percentage of blacks in the armed forces—approximately 19.6 percent as of June, 1993—whereas Dorn's statement, reported above, that if there had been a long ground war in Iraq some one-fourth of casualties would have been black, related this figure to the black percentage of the U.S. population—12 percent.

ropean component and by the NAACP national office in Balti-
more, Maryland. A team composed of NAACP officials including John J. Johnson, director of Armed Services and Veterans
Affairs for the NAACP, and James D. Williams, director of
public relations, visited 5 military bases in Germany in November, 1992. A report by Williams in the NAACP magazine *Crisis*
stated that "with the cooperation of the Department of Defense"
the group held public hearings at four Army bases and one Air Force
base in Germany. They heard from more that 250 individuals including officers, enlisted personnel and civilian employees.

"The accounts shared with the NAACP hearing panel ranged
across a wide spectrum of complaints including allegations of
unequal discipline, unjust reductions in rank and assignment,
improper and/or lengthy handling of equal opportunity complaints, reprisals for speaking up, unwarranted separations from
service, mistreatment by military police and failure to secure
promotions," Williams wrote.

Citing several cases of alleged discrimination against individual black military personnel, Williams stated:

"Out of these hearings came a veritable mountain of information which will serve as the basis of a report on the equal opportunity climate for African-Americans overseas.... The report will
include findings and recommendations."

It is worthy of note that, in two of four specific cases cited in
the article, the alleged discriminatory actions were later reversed
in whole or in large part. While the article does not say so, there
is an inference that NAACP interest in the two cases played a
part in the reversal.

Referring to the segregation of black service personnel during
World War II, Williams wrote:

"The treatment accorded the black soldiers back then stands in stark contrast to what is going on today, where the fault lies not so much in the intent of the Pentagon to do the right thing, but the implementation of policies when it gets down to the individual."

In a final statement before leaving Germany, the NAACP task force said:

"It is to the military's credit that it has been so cooperative during the visit. We are under no illusion that without the cooperation, this visit could not have been as productive as it was....We recognize that in a time of such sweeping changes as the military is currently experiencing, there are many pressing problems that must be resolved. Nevertheless we firmly believe that equal opportunity in the military must remain as a high priority and we will not relent in our efforts to ensure that it does." (That statement was quoted in Williams' article.)

Civil Rights Commission Chairman Arthur Fletcher's reports on alleged anti-black discrimination were based on trips he made to Germany in 1991 and to Japan in March 1993. He said that his findings were his own and not those of the Civil Rights Commission, an eight-member independent agency of the executive branch. Four of its members are appointed by the president and four by Congress. Dr. Fletcher, Distinguished Professor of Business Administration and Director of the Center for Corporate Social Policy at the University of Denver, Colorado, was appointed to the chairmanship by President Bush for a five-year term ending in 1995.

Dr. Fletcher did not say why, in his public statements and his comments to this author, he emphasized that his findings were his alone and not those of the Commission. He did say, in a press conference following his tour of military bases in Germany in 1991, that he "will be briefing the Commission" on the contents of his report on his tour; and he stated that written complaints received as a result of his trips to bases in Germany were being reviewed by the Commission staff.

In the press conference regarding his tour of U.S. military bases in Germany, which took place at the National Press Club in Washington, D.C., Sept. 11, 1991, Dr. Fletcher said that during his trip he "saw much that was commendable in the efficiency of the base operations and the calibre of the personnel. Clearly, the key leadership of the U.S. military intends to root out all vestiges of discrimination in the armed services. The problem appears to be that they haven't done it yet, and a great many Americans in uniform and their families are hurting because of that."

He said his was "not a U.S. Commission on Civil Rights-sponsored trip, the report is not a Commission report, and this is not a Commission-hosted press conference. The contents of the report are mine and mine alone." He stated that written complaints of civil rights violations in the U.S. military in Germany, analyzed thus far by the Commission staff, "strengthen my belief that there is a strong perception by African American servicemen and servicewomen in Germany that:

• "they are disciplined more readily than white service persons;

• "they received lower officer evaluations merely because they are black;

• "the military community, as a whole, in Germany treats blacks with 'disdain'; and

• "the Commanders on the military bases appear to reinforce negative racial stereotypes against black soldiers."

He added that the complaints "lend credence to my earlier

statement that the DoD [Defense Department] school system in Germany seems to be failing black youth—the same way it is failing them in the U.S. For example, a complaint that was analyzed by staff demonstrated that black military parents are 'insulted and treated like children when they inquire about the unfair treatment of their children in the military school system.'"

He said the preliminary finding in employment complaints was that, "'Black civilians are still the last hired and the first fired,' and if hired, are usually denied access to higher level positions within DoD."

"I continue to believe that the senior military staff has a high level of interest in becoming more aware of the discrimination experienced by our troops and civilian military personnel overseas, and that we can begin to work together to rectify these problems," he said.

In what he labelled his "preliminary report" on his 1991 fact-finding European trip, Dr. Fletcher said there was "proof to indicate breaches of the civil rights of United States citizens serving within the United States military" or who are "civilian employees within the Department of Defense in Europe." His report dealt with civil rights practices in schools for dependents of military personnel, civilian employees of the military, evaluation boards and promotional systems, and the military justice system.

On April 29, 1993, Dr. Fletcher sent a letter to President Clinton reiterating and adding to his charges of racial *and gender* discrimination in the U.S. military, including his findings on a trip he made to military bases in Japan in the spring of 1993.

He said that on his trip to Germany he found "double standards and blatant, racial and gender discrimination being practiced throughout the European command."

"It saddens me to say so, but in some cases it actually appeared that such behavior was being sanctioned by base commanders and their subordinates with a vengeance," he wrote the president. "Not only did I find that to be the case in Germany, but throughout the entire United States from Alaska to Florida, from California to Maine and all points in between; service segment not withstanding. By that I mean the Army, Air Force, Navy and the Marine Corps."

He said records in his office "will show that Tailhook [the 1992 Navy sex harassment scandal] was anything but an aberration—it is a culture, an everyday way of life in all four service branches that minorities and women endure, day in and day out. I know that the above sounds like a sweeping allegation, but I will challenge the Congress, the White House, or both to appoint an independent investigating team to unearth the facts and prove that I have overstated the case."

Dr. Fletcher said, in his letter to President Clinton, that he had visited Japan in early March, 1993, and found "blatant racism, genderism and discrimination in spades at each of the three bases I visited. The charges were the same. The military, the civil service system, and the DODDS [schools for children of military personnel]...were polluted with the toxic practices of racism, genderism and ethnic discrimination."

He began his letter to President Clinton by asking the president's "immediate attention" to the case of T/Sgt. Arthur W. Diggs, a member of the Air Force in California, who claimed discrimination in a letter to Dr. Fletcher. The Civil Rights Commission chairman included with his letter numerous documents supporting his charges of discrimination at U.S. military bases in Japan.

He told President Clinton that, "in writing this letter and forwarding these materials, I am speaking for myself only; therefore the views expressed are mine and mine alone. Thus, I did not seek clearance from any of the other commissioners in drafting and submitting this request for your direct intervention in this matter [of T/Sgt. Diggs]." He sent copies of his letter to Secretary of Defense Les Aspin, Gen. Colin Powell, Chairman of the Joint Chiefs of Staff, the secretaries of the Army, Air Force and Navy and the Marine Corps commandant, to several members of Congress and to other organizations and individuals including the NAACP and the Urban League.

(Dr. Fletcher's complaints and charges, with supporting material, were made available to this author by Dr. Fletcher's office in Washington at his direction. As of the time this book went to press, the author had been unable to obtain any reaction from the White House to Dr. Fletcher's letter. Charles Pei Wang, vice chairman of the Civil Rights Commission, told the author in mid-1993 that Dr. Fletcher had briefed the Commission on his findings, but that the Commission had not taken up the issue of discrimination in the armed forces as a body. He said that the Commission's agenda was filled for 1993, and in addition its budget had been reduced by Congress. A staff member of the Commision said that complaints received by the Commission about cases of discrimination had been forwarded to the Equal Opportunity Office of the Defense Department. The author was unable, in the time available, to learn the ultimate disposition of the complaints.)

***

In the spring of 1993 I submitted a questionnaire to a "Congressional Staff Source" with responsibility for monitoring the situation of blacks in the military, and who examines complaints of discrimination. Asked about the present status of racial integration in the military as regards recruitment, training, duty, combat, use of facilities such as eating, sleeping, etc., and whether there are any barriers to utilization of black manpower, this source stated:

"The United States military is one of the most integrated institutions in America today. There are no restrictions on recruiting, training, duty, combat, or use of facilities. There have not been any barriers to utilization of Negro manpower for a number of years, perhaps since the Korean War."

Asked if there are still problems with off-duty racial mixing on or off military bases, the source replied:

"There are no problems with off-duty race mixing on base or off base. However there is still a propensity for people to go on liberty with members of their own race. Social clubs and dances on bases are mixed and a variety of music is played."

Are there problems with African American servicemen and women and nearby communities?

"Yes. There are still isolated cases of housing discrimination but I do not think it is widespread. The local base commander can declare housing units or other public establishments off limits to all military personnel if an establishment does not rent or cater to personnel of all races. The most recent case of housing discrimination that comes to mind was in Maryland, near Andrews Air Force Base, and was reported in the *Washington Post* several months ago."

Is there friction among African Americans and whites in the military serious enough to be reported to the Pentagon?

"There are cases that are reported to the Pentagon. However I would not put them in the serious category. These cases are sent

242

to the inspector generals of the various services for investigation and action."

Are there complaints about the treatment of African Americans from individuals within the military, and from outside organizations and individuals?

"There are numerous complaints from individuals within the military, and from outside organizations such as the Southern Christian Leadership Conference and the National Association for the Advancement of Colored People. These complaints are allegations of discrimination and unfair treatment in evaluations, promotions and assignments. These cases are also sent to the inspector generals of the various services for investigation and action."

Are there problems with blacks coming into the military in numbers disproportionate to their numbers in the society at large?

I do not consider this a problem during the current downsizing [reduction in size of the armed forces]. In the past blacks entered the military in large numbers because this was their quickest route into the mainstream of American society. Many joined for the GI Bill benefits while others came in search of careers. There have been recent indications from the services that the propensity for blacks to serve has decreased from previous years." (The latter was reported also by Dr. Milton Morris of the Joint Center for Political and Economic Studies.)

Are blacks being killed at a disproportionate rate in armed conflict?

"This proved not to be the case in the Persian Gulf War. However there were relatively few casualties in that war and it may not be a good conflict to use to make the point."

I asked the Congressional staff source whether blacks are more likely than whites to volunteer for military service.

"In the past blacks had a greater propensity to serve in the military because of the military's record on equal opportunity and upward mobility for blacks. During this period of downsizing there are indications that the propensity of blacks to serve has decreased somewhat."

Finally, in my interview in early June with Dr. Milton D. Morris, Vice President for Research of the Joint Center for Political and Economic Studies, he said he keeps tabs on the situation of blacks in the military from three sources: armed services data, which he termed "most consistent and credible"; academic literature on the subject; and opinion surveys including some of his own. He has testified on this issue before the House of Representatives Veterans Affairs Subcommittee.

He said that, over time, there has been "profound ambivalence" of the black population towards the military, and to the experience of black soldiers. He said that, in his testimony before the Veterans Affairs Subcommittee, he discussed the ambivalence of the black population toward Desert Storm—one side being blacks' right to serve "as an affirmation of their equality."

"Hence," he told me, "there is a very strong pursuit among blacks of access to the military. There has been some question about whether blacks should serve in the military—whether they are exploited. The ambivalence has persisted. During Desert Storm there were a lot of claims by the black leadership that it was bad policy, that blacks were going to be a disproportionate share of victims, etc.; that they were not really true volunteers, but were forced by economic circumstances to volunteer for the military. There is a disproportionate number of blacks in the military; and a disproportion in front-line combat units—as high as 30 percent in some units.

"I've gone through all the data—accessions, retention, distribution up the ranks. We find a very high proportion of black soldiers who feel their careers are performance-driven, not racially. It is most positive in a number of surveys. Black high school people have had a very high propensity to serve until very recently. In the wake of Desert Storm I have been told there has been a recent decline in the propensity to enlist by all segments of society, and a sharper decline among black youths.

"I see the military as a very encouraging case in support of basic American values. They offer the benefit of diversity and the possibility of constructively dealing with diversity. The military may point the way to society at large on some late stage of race relations. We are not dealing with segregation but equal opportunity."

Dr. Morris said that a recent study by a researcher in the Joint Center for Political and Economic Studies shows that the downsizing of the military, "while it hurts all, is not disproportionately hard on blacks; it's slightly better. I see this as a tribute to management in the process. The downsized military in its racial composition looks very much like the military prior to downsizing."

I asked Dr. Morris if there was criticism of the situation of blacks in the military.

"There are still substantial numbers of individual cases involving claims of discrimination in some theaters more than others, such as Europe," he said. "I don't see any major institutional criticism or complaints. I see particular problems tied to particular locations. By and large I don't see any systematic racial problems. The officer ranks are very unequal in terms of minority representation. This is not a major source of complaint about the policy."

According to the *Army Times* of Feb. 8, 1993, the Minority Officers Association, a non-profit lobby group based in California, has been asking Congress since 1988 to create "a military civil rights commission" outside the regular chain of command. Retired Maj. Aristides Gonzales, the group's spokesman, told the *Army Times*, "As a former personnel and equal opportunity officer, I understand where the glitches are. People in the services will tell you: You just have to hunker down and take it because the moment you complain, the roof falls in on you."

The *Army Times* said that Gonzales retired in 1985 after an unsuccessful attempt to sue the Army over not being promoted to lieutenant colonel.

I have attempted, in this somewhat over-long essay, to make up for my lack of time and opportunity to do independent research on the current status of blacks in the U.S. military— such as I did in writing my original book in 1952-53. My own conclusion is that the present policy of equality of opportunity for blacks in the military is firm, service-wide and generally well enforced. There are evidently many claims of anti-black discrimination, and this author cannot address the effectiveness of the military's efforts to deal with them on a fair and equitable basis.

I close with a quotation from Col. Ronald Joe, head of the Defense Equal Opportunity Management Institute at Andrews Air Force Base in Florida. In answer to one of my questions (as quoted in Appendix A) he said:

"The Defense Department is clearly a leader [in promoting equal opportunity]. There is still a lot to do. We have to continue to work on all important issues: race, sexism, religious intolerance, women. There has been a lot of progress but we must continue across the entire range to work at constant improvement to make sure our forces are ready from a human relations standpoint."

Appendix D

Question and Answer With a Staff Representative of the
Department of Defense (DoD) Equal Opportunity (EO) Office to Author's Questionnaire

Q: Are there any all-African American units still in existence in the U.S. armed services?

A: No.

Q: When was the last all-black unit abolished?

A: 1954.

Q: Are there any off-duty or social problems for blacks in the military?

A: Not on any large scale. The only off-duty problems might be discrimination in off-base housing. I'm not aware of any large-scale problems. There may have been isolated incidences of off-duty civilian-military relations.

Q: What about problems with nearby communities?

A: I've not seen anything significant since the 1980s. Anything now is of an individual nature.

Q: Is there any black-white friction serious enough to be reported to the Pentagon?

A: Not that I'm aware of. In the Persian Gulf war, nothing of that nature came out of it; no reported friction between blacks and whites.

Q: Are there complaints within the military or from outside sources?

A: Individuals have submitted complaints to the DoD and they are being looked at. All are of an individual nature. The issue of off-base housing discrimination has pretty much gone away.

Q: Do you have any information about impact of the military EO program on civilian society in the U.S.?

A: In DoD's equal opportunity programs, civilian and military EO staffs work separately but do similar work. On some installations they support each other on common projects such as Black History Month observances. One recent impact on private sector equal opportunity is that the Defense Equal Opportunity Management Institute (DEOMI) has been approached by the Russian Republic on ethnic relations (see comments by Col. Ronald Joe, head of DEOMI, in Appendix A.) DEOMI has received inquiries from private corporations who want their equal opportunity people to go through that school. During the Black Power movement in the 1970s, civilian civil rights issues spilled over to the military. There was a Black Power movement in the military—Black Power salutes etc.

Q: Are there any barriers to assigning black personnel anywhere in the world?

A: Race is not a factor in assigning personnel. Blacks can go
      anywhere, as far as I know. There are bound to be black
      personnel in any organization over 10-15 personnel.

Q: What about Dr. Dorn's statement that there are "vestiges"
      of discrimination in the armed forces? (This refers to a
      statement by Dr. Edwin B. Dorn, then a senior staff mem-
      ber of Brookings Institution, to a subcommittee of the
      House of Representatives Armed Services Committee July
      29, 1992, in which Dr. Dorn said that, "Even today, there
      are problems with the vestiges of societal discrimination
      that cause blacks and other minorities to be concentrated
      disproportionately in administration and in supply jobs in
      the services, and to be underrepresented in the officer corps,
      particularly in the Navy's officer corps." In other testimony
      before the House Armed Services Committee and its sub-
      committees, Dr. Dorn had mostly positive things to say
      about the situation of blacks in today's military (see Ap-
      pendix C). He is currently Assistant Secretary of Defense
      for Personnel and Readiness.

A: There is a concerted effort to do something to eliminate
      them (vestiges of discrimination). Every service has an affir-
      mative action plan. They document and identify EO prob-
      lems. Every year there is an analysis of these EO problems,
      with copies sent to the DoD EO Office.

Q: What about disproportionate representation of minorities,
      especially blacks, in the officer corps?

A: DoD takes steps to increase recruiting [of blacks]. Recruit-
      ing ads are placed in black magazines such as *Ebony, Jet* and
      others. Recruiting teams are sent to colleges and universi-
      ties; when they find qualified minorities, they talk to them.

Retention has become a problem. There is an effort to retain qualified technically trained personnel, regardless of race, in a number of areas. There is overrepresentation of blacks in courts-martial convictions. We don't know the reason. There are some studies by the services. DEOMI is coordinating a service-wide study.

Q: What is the Defense Department policy on segregation?

A: There is no specific document on non-segregation by race or national origin; but it is firm DoD policy that discrimination of any form in any aspect of military life should not exist and will not be tolerated. Segregation as a word is no longer used. You can say it, but Equal Opportunity is our term now.